DATE		

8-05

DISCOVERY & EXPLORATION

Across America:
The Lewis and Clark Expedition

MAURICE ISSERMAN

JOHN S. BOWMAN and MAURICE ISSERMAN
General Editors

☑®
Facts On File, Inc.

Across America: The Lewis and Clark Expedition

Facts On File, Inc.
132 West 31st Street
New York NY 10001

Library of Congress Cataloging-in-Publication Data

Isserman, Maurice.
     Across America : the Lewis and Clark expedition / Maurice Isserman.
          v. cm. —(Discovery and exploration)
          Contents: Monticello and Lemhi Pass, August 12, 1805—Search for the North-
     west Passage—Preparing the way, March 1803–May 1804—Up the Missouri,
     May–October 1804—"The most perfect harmoney": winter at Fort Mandan—
     "This little fleet": up the unknown Missouri—To the Missouri headwaters—On
     foot and on horse across the Rockies—"Ocean in view!": to the Pacific—Home-
     ward bound.
     ISBN 0-8160-5256-5
          1. Lewis and Clark Expedition (1804–1806)—Juvenile literature. 2. West
     (U.S.)—Discovery and exploration—Juvenile literature. 3. West (U.S.)—Des-
     cription and travel—Juvenile literature. [Lewis and Clark Expedition
     (1804–1806) 2. Explorers. 3. West (U.S.)—Discovery and exploration. 4. West
     (U.S.)—Description and travel.] I. Title. II. Series.
     F592.7. I87 2004
     917. 804'2—dc22   2003025130

Facts On File books are available at special discounts when purchased in bulk
quantities for businesses, associations, institutions, or sales promotions. Please
call our Special Sales Department in New York at (212) 967-8800 or (800) 322-8755.

You can find Facts On File on the World Wide Web at
http://www.factsonfile.com

Text design by Erika K. Arroyo
Cover design by Kelly Parr
Maps by Pat Meschino

Printed in the United States of America

VB FOF 10 9 8 7 6 5 4 3 2 1

This book is printed on acid-free paper.

For David Weintraub,
who for 30 years has been Lewis to my Clark,
and Clark to my Lewis.

Note on Photos

Many of the illustrations and photographs used in this book are old, historical images. The quality of the prints is not always up to current standards, as in some cases the originals are from old or poor quality negatives or are damaged. The content of the illustrations, however, made their inclusion important despite problems in reproduction.

CONTENTS

INTRODUCTION

On April 7, 1805, Captain Meriwether Lewis dipped his pen in ink and made an entry in a red leather-bound notebook. Since the previous May, he and the men under his command had traveled 1,600 miles by boat up the Missouri River. They were known as the Corps of Discovery. They had spent the winter of 1804–05 in a little wooden fort that they constructed at a site near present-day Bismarck, North Dakota. The ice on the river had finally melted, and they were preparing to resume their journey. As Lewis surveyed the six small canoes and two larger boats called pirogues that would carry his party westward to the farthest reaches of the Missouri River, he voiced a deep sense of satisfaction. "This little fleet," Lewis wrote in his journal that day, "altho' not quite so rispectable as those of Columbus or Capt. Cook, were still viewed by us with as much pleasure as those deservedly famed adventurers ever beheld theirs. . . ."

Two hundred years later, Lewis and Clark's "little fleet" is itself "deservedly famed" in the annals of exploration and discovery. Larry McMurtry, a Pulitzer prize–winning novelist, recently described the journey of the Corps of Discovery as "our first really American adventure," and its record in the pages of the journals kept by Meriwether Lewis and his co-commander William Clark as "our only really American epic."

What places Lewis and Clark in the first rank of American explorers? They led the first

A U.S. Army captain, Meriwether Lewis left active military duty to assist President Jefferson in secretarial tasks. His acute awareness and attention to detail were an asset to the president and proved useful again in Lewis's journal entries and drawings. *(Library of Congress, Prints and Photographs Division [LC-USZ62-10609])*

exploration party ever officially sponsored by the government of the United States. They were the first white men, and very likely the first men ever to cross the entire North American continent through the territory that would soon become the western United States. They were the first white men to travel on the Missouri River in the territory that was to become the state of Montana, and thus the first to see the Great Falls of Montana, the Gates of the Rockies, the Three Forks of the Missouri, and the river's headwaters in the Rocky Mountains. They were the first white men to cross the Continental Divide south of Canada, the first white men to explore the length of the Yellowstone River, the first white men to see the Clearwater and Snake Rivers, and the first white men to sail down the Columbia River to the sea. They were the first white men to make direct contact with and learn something about the life of the Shoshone, the Flathead (Salish), and the Nez Perce Indian tribes. They discovered and were the first to describe for scientific purposes 122 species of western birds and animals and 178 plants. They left their names, and the names of the members of the Corps of Discovery, on hundreds of hills, rivers, creeks, and cities throughout the Great Plains and Pacific Northwest regions of the United States.

But beyond the many "firsts" that can be listed next to their names, Lewis and Clark deserve their ranking among the greatest of American explorers because of the personal qualities that they displayed on their expedition. They were exemplary explorers. It is not just that they were men of "undaunted courage," as historian Stephen Ambrose called them, though they certainly were that. Their greatest virtues as explorers proved to be their power of observation and their rarely waning enthusiasm for, as Lewis put it, the "scenes of visionary enchantment" that they

encountered on their long journey to the Pacific and back.

Biologist Paul Cutright wrote in *Lewis and Clark, Pioneering Naturalists* that Meriwether Lewis possessed an ability "effortlessly and spontaneously" to see the "little things so often overlooked, even by the well-trained naturalist." Historian James Ronda, in *Lewis and Clark among the Indians*, praised Lewis's abilities as an ethnographer (someone who studies human cultures and races); Lewis, Ronda wrote, had "the naturalist's ability to describe objects with almost photographic fidelity. [He] brought to ethnography the practiced eye of one who delighted in describing and cataloguing the creatures of the natural world." Mapmaking, or cartography, is a craft that depends upon close observation and measurement: Geologist John Logan Allen wrote in *Lewis and Clark and the Image of the American Northwest* that William Clark proved himself "a cartographer of unusual skill" whose maps of the Missouri and Columbia basins were "cartographic masterpieces."

Lewis and Clark were also, as historian Donald Jackson once famously noted, the "writingest explorers." Among the tons of supplies the explorers carried with them were, as listed in their inventories "6 papers of ink powder" and "4 metal pens brass or silver." Following instructions given to Lewis by President Thomas Jefferson, Lewis, Clark, and at least six other members of the expedition kept journals. Taken together, these journals allow people today to reconstruct on a day-by-day basis, from May 14, 1804, to September 23, 1806, where the explorers were, how far they traveled, what they were doing, what they were eating, how their health was holding up, and the state of their morale.

Lewis and Clark were the most prolific of the journal-keepers: Between the two of them they produced 200,000 words in the

Throughout the journey, Lewis and Clark encountered many unfamiliar plants and animals. They carefully described their findings in their journals and demonstrated great talent in cartography (mapmaking) and drawing. This illustration is one Clark made of the sage grouse, a bird Lewis dubbed "mountain cock," "heath cock," and "cock of the plains." *(Missouri Historical Society)* time it took them to make the round-trip from St. Louis, Missouri, to the Pacific Ocean. When one thinks of the Lewis and Clark expedition, one tends to remember the great moments of discovery: Lewis standing atop Lemhi Pass on the Continental Divide, Clark recording his joy at his first view of the Pacific, both men marveling at the sight of thousands of buffalo spread out across the Great Plains landscape, and so on. To those images another should be added: the captains sitting with their little portable wooden desks spread out on their laps after a long, hard, and often dangerous day's travel, sitting by the campfire and writing, writing, writing in their journals.

It is not only the quantity but the quality of their writing that makes the Lewis and Clark journals a continuing source of fascination to Americans, an "American epic," in Larry McMurtry's words. Though Lewis and Clark had no intention of creating great literature when they set down the record of the expedition, in McMurtry's opinion, "by the force and immediacy of the expression, they accomplished the one essential thing that writers must do: they brought the reader along with them, up that meandering river and over those snowy peaks." And, as Lewis's biographer Stephen Ambrose commented with equal admiration, "On virtually every page they reveal something of their personalities." The words that Lewis and Clark and other members of the expedition recorded between 1804 and 1806 lie at the heart of the narrative that follows. All quotations, except where otherwise noted, come from Lewis's or Clark's pen.

A note on spelling: By Larry McMurtry's estimate, William Clark found 22 different ways to spell the word *Sioux* in the journals. He probably came up with almost as many variations in spelling the word *mosquito.*

William Clark joined the expedition when he received the offer directly from fellow Virginian and fellow officer Meriwether Lewis. *(Library of Congress, Prints and Photographs Division [LC-USZ62-105848])*

Lewis came closer to standard spelling, but as his rendering of the word *"rispectable"* [respectable] in the sentence that describes his "little fleet" suggests, he was not always successful. In the account that follows, the original spelling has been left intact in the quotations. Where the meaning of a word may be unclear, the version set down by Lewis and Clark will be followed by the correctly spelled word in brackets. The quotations from the journals are all taken from Gary Moulton's recent and definitive edition of *The Journals of the Lewis and Clark Expedition,* published in 13 volumes by the University of Nebraska Press.

1

MONTICELLO AND LEMHI PASS

August 12, 1805

 The president of the United States, Thomas Jefferson, was spending the summer of 1805 at Monticello, his stately hilltop home in Virginia's Piedmont region. There, amid the tranquil beauties of his plantation's flower and herb gardens, he was able to escape for a while the pressures of office, as well as the heat, humidity, dust, and disease that the summer months brought to the nation's new capital in Washington, D.C. So Jefferson was not at the White House on Monday, August 12, 1805, when a long-expected wagonload of wooden boxes, trunks, and cages arrived there for him.

The shipment included animal skins, skeletons, antlers and horns, minerals, seeds, dried plants, a tin box containing insects and mice, a buffalo robe painted with the scene of a battle fought by American Indian tribes, an Indian bow and quiver of arrows, a live magpie, and a something described on the list accompanying the shipment as a "living burrowing squirrel of the praries" (better known today as a

prairie dog). This odd assortment had been packaged and sent to Jefferson four months earlier by his young friend and former aide Captain Meriwether Lewis of the U.S. Army.

Lewis had dispatched the shipment from his temporary base at Fort Mandan on the upper Missouri River, near the junction of the Missouri and the Knife Rivers in the present-day state of North Dakota, a place that in the winter of 1804–05 had represented the westernmost outpost of the authority of the government of the United States. From Fort Mandan, the boxes and crates had followed a circuitous route to their final destination at Jefferson's official residence. They were carried by boat down the Missouri River to St. Louis, then down the Mississippi River to New Orleans, then by sea to Baltimore, and finally by wagon to the White House.

President Jefferson did not have a chance to examine the contents of Lewis's shipment for several months, but he was delighted to hear of their arrival. He instructed his servants

1

at the White House to make sure that the skins and furs were well preserved and that the magpie and prairie dog were looked after (they were still alive when he got back to Washington in October). He also looked forward to the day when he would be able to hear firsthand from Captain Lewis about his adventures, but he knew it would be many months, perhaps even a year, before that would be possible. For Meriwether Lewis and the small party of explorers that he led were at that moment somewhere deep in the American western wilderness, traversing a blank place on the existing maps of the North American continent, where non-Indian Americans had never before ventured.

Thomas Jefferson held many important political positions in his life, most notably that of the third president of the United States. But he was also an inventor, a naturalist, a linguist, an architect, the author of the Declaration of Independence, and the founder of the University of Virginia. Jefferson worked to organize the exploration of a Northwest Passage for 20 years before finally succeeding. *(National Archives [NWDNS-208-PU-104HH(4)])*

THAT SAME DAY, ABOUT 1,850 MILES WEST OF MONTICELLO . . .

On August 12, 1805, Lewis awoke early. He was an impressive-looking man, more than six feet tall, lean and well muscled, his skin deeply tanned by the sun. He was camped with three other men by a small stream near the western border of the present-day state of Montana, a stream that he believed would lead them in a day or so to the headwaters of the Missouri River. The rest of his expedition, laden with supplies that they were transporting in dugout canoes, was following more slowly 20 or so miles behind Lewis and the advance party. Lewis and his companions were traveling light, on foot, with no provisions but what they could carry on their back. They had no tent and slept under the stars, wrapped in their blankets. But they did have an American flag, which flew over their small camp on a wooden pole that Lewis stuck in the ground the night before.

At first light Captain Lewis sent George Drouillard, a civilian hunter, one of the most competent men under his command, to look for the trail of an Indian whom they had spotted the day before. Lewis hoped that this Indian was a Shoshone and could lead them to the rest of his tribe. Ever since their departure from Fort Mandan in April they had looked forward to meeting the Shoshone, because they had heard it was a tribe rich in horses. Lewis and his party would need horses to carry their supplies over the Rocky Mountains to the headwaters of the Columbia River, which they believed lay just on the other side.

Thomas Jefferson designed this stately home for himself in 1768. Monticello stands near Charlottesville, Virginia, and is a popular tourist attraction for visitors to the area. *(Library of Congress, Prints and Photographs Division [LC-USZ62-107586])*

Once they were on the Columbia they could build new canoes and sail down to the Pacific Ocean, their ultimate goal.

It was still early morning when Drouillard returned. The rain the night before made it hard to find the Indian's trail. Still they decided to press on up a gentle valley that led them to a high wooded hillside. The stream they had camped along branched into smaller rivulets. As always, Lewis kept his eyes open for unfamiliar plant and animal life, whose distinguishing features he carefully noted in his journal. He noted "several large hawks" that flew overhead, "nearly black in color" (possibly red-tailed hawks, or Swaison's

hawks). Later he saw a large animal "of the fox kind" (probably a wolverine). There were also signs of Indian presence; the ground by the stream had been dug up by Shoshone searching for edible roots. Later in the morning Lewis and his party stopped to rest and breakfasted on the last of the dried deer meat that they were carrying in their packs; they had no other food with them except a small amount of salt pork and some flour.

They had found an Indian path that led them up the valley, until it turned "abruptly to the West through a narrow bottom betwen the mountains." The path was getting steeper, but they pushed on, their excitement mounting.

Thomas Jefferson's Other Explorers ⟋

Lewis and Clark's lasting fame, although certainly justified, has obscured the efforts of the other explorers who headed west in the years of Thomas Jefferson's presidency. Jefferson saw the Lewis and Clark expedition as just one part of a multipronged and coordinated effort to learn more about the vast region of western North America. When Jefferson reported in February 1806 on Lewis and Clark's progress up the Missouri (based on information the two expedition leaders had sent back to Washington from their first winter encampment in North Dakota), he did so in a document entitled "Message from the President of the United States Communicating Discoveries Made in Exploring the Missouri, Red River, and Washita, by Captains Lewis and Clarke, Doctor Sibley, and Mr. Dunbar."

At Jefferson's request, William Dunbar, a Mississippi planter, and George Hunter, a Philadelphia chemist, led an expedition up the Ouchita River through northern Louisiana into present-day Arkansas in fall 1804. In spring 1805 a second Jefferson expedition set off up the Red River, this one led by Thomas Freeman, a civil engineer and surveyor, and Thomas Custis, a medical student. Dr. John Sibley joined them en route. Their 40-man expedition pushed up the Red River into present-day Texas, then part of the Spanish empire in the New World. On July 29, Spanish troops intercepted the American explorers at a spot on the Red River known ever since as Spanish Bluff, about 30 miles northwest of present-day Texarkana, Texas. The Spanish commander bluntly told them that they had to return to where they came from or be taken into custody.

After Lewis and Clark, the best-known explorer of Jefferson's era was undoubtedly another army officer, Lt. Zebulon Montgomery Pike. Pike was born in Lamberton, New Jersey, in 1779, the son of an American military officer. Following his father's example, Zebulon joined the U.S. Army at the age of 15, and he served on the Ohio frontier in the 1790s. In July 1806 Pike led an expeditionary party west from St. Louis, up the Missouri River, then along the Arkansas River, and finally, on horseback, crossing the Kansas plains into Colorado. There they were the first Americans to encounter the Front Range of the Colorado Rockies. (One of those peaks has since been known as Pike's Peak.) Like the Freeman expedition, Pike's party ran into Spanish troops, who put them under arrest for trespassing onto Spanish lands. Pike and some of his men were released to U.S. authorities in Louisiana on June 30, 1807. Other members of the party were later released. "Language cannot express the gaiety of my heart when I once beheld the standards of my country waved aloft," Pike said of his return.

"[T]he road was still plain," Lewis wrote in his journal soon afterward, "I therefore did not dispair of shortly finding a passage over the mountains and of taisting the waters of the great Columbia this evening." Up and up they walked, four more miles, until finally they

Painted in 1988 by Robert F. Morgan, *At Lemhi* shows Lewis joined by three other members of the expedition, taking a moment's rest as they searched for the Shoshone Indians in July 1805. *(Montana Historical Society, Helena)*

came to the spring bubbling up from the ground that fed the little stream (present-day Trail Creek) they walked alongside. This, Lewis believed, was "the most distant fountain of mighty Missouri in surch of which we have spent so many toilsome days and wristless nights." One of his men, Hugh McNeal, stood with one foot planted "on each side of this little rivulet and," Lewis noted, McNeal had "thanked his god that he had lived to bestride the mighty & heretofore deemed endless Missouri." As for Lewis, his joy knew no bounds: "I had accomplished one of those great objects on which my mind has been unalterably fixed for many years . . ." He asked any future readers of his journal to "judge then of the pleas-

ure I felt in allaying my thirst with this pure and ice cold water," the headwaters or origin of the Missouri River.

It was another half-mile to the summit. The pass ahead, later to be known as Lemhi Pass, crossed the Continental Divide. On the eastern side of the mountains, all waters flowed east or southward, eventually to end up in the Mississippi River and the Gulf of Mexico. On the western side, which they were approaching, all waters would eventually flow by one means or another to the Pacific. And that included the Columbia River, whose headwaters Lewis fully expected to find on the far slope. No non-Indian American had ever before stepped across the Continental Divide.

Finally they were at the top, 7,373 feet above sea level, with a broad vista opening up to the west. And there, "from the top of the divideing ridge," there was no sign of the Columbia River and the easy water route that they had dreamed of finding to the Pacific. Instead, as Lewis wrote, "I discovered immence ranges of high mountains still to the West of us with their tops partially covered with snow." They were at the farthest boundary of the United States. They had a long, hard way to go before they would see the Pacific Ocean.

2

SEARCH FOR THE NORTHWEST PASSAGE

The New World that Christopher Columbus encountered in 1492 represented both an opportunity and an obstacle to European explorers and to the soldiers, missionaries, traders, and settlers who would follow in their paths. Columbus had been searching for an old, not a new, continent. He had hoped to find a passage to the riches of Asia, an ocean crossing to replace the long, difficult land route that in past centuries had brought a mere trickle of trade goods from India and China to European markets. Instead, he stumbled upon the Americas—two continents previously unknown to Europeans, home to tens of millions of Native peoples whose civilizations would in time be swept aside by the conquering powers from across the Atlantic. There were riches in the Americas: gold, silver, and timber; rich fishing grounds off the coasts; endless lands where European settlers could grow cotton, rice, wheat, and corn; and pastures and plains where they could graze their sheep, cows, and horses. But for all the potential bounty of the New World, the Americas also stood in the way of the realization of the European quest to find a waterborne trade route to Asia, to India and China—fabled and distant lands of silks and spices.

Nevertheless, the dream of what the European explorers called the "passage to India" proved hard to kill. It took new form in the belief that, somewhere, the American continents must be pierced by a water route—a strait, or perhaps a great inland sea that drained to both the Atlantic and the Pacific, or, failing that, a system of rivers that could be linked together by short portages where small boats could be carried across land from one body of navigable water to the next. For the next three centuries after Columbus's landing in the New World, generation after generation of European explorers sought that elusive water route across the Americas.

In the course of the 16th century, Spanish and Portuguese explorers were able to establish that neither South nor Central America offered such a route. That left North America.

Unlike the regions to the south that had been claimed by Spain and Portugal, the interior regions of North America and its western coastline remained largely unexplored and unsettled by Europeans and their American descendants century after century. The enticing possibility of finding a "Northwest Passage" through the Arctic regions of the North American continent or through some combination of rivers, lakes, and inland seas in the interior of the continent, excited the imagination of European explorers such as John Cabot, Giovanni da Verrazano, Jacques Cartier, Samuel de Champlain, and Henry Hudson in the 16th and 17th centuries. They never found the opening to the Pacific that they sought so diligently, but the discoveries they made in the course of their search for the Northwest Passage helped lay the groundwork for the great rival North American empires of Britain and France.

THE MISSOURI:
Key to the Northwest Passage?

In the 17th and 18th centuries, the French accomplished many of the boldest and most successful journeys of exploration in the North American interior. In 1673, French-Canadian explorer Louis Joliet and Jesuit missionary Jacques Marquette, accompanied by five *voyageurs* (boatmen skilled in wilderness travel), sailed from Canada down the Mississippi River as far south as present-day Arkansas. Along the way they came upon the mouth of a large river that emptied into the Mississippi, a river previously unknown to Europeans. This river, eventually named the Missouri after a local Indian tribe, proved to be the principal tributary of the Mississippi.

After his return to Canada, Father Marquette would describe the Missouri as a river "of considerable size, coming from the north-west, from a great distance." How great a distance, he could not tell, but later explorers would establish its length some 2,464 miles from its headwaters to its mouth, making it the longest river in North America. The Missouri drains a river basin of more than 500,000 square miles, and it includes among its own tributaries such mighty and fabled American rivers as the Yellowstone, the Grand, the Heart, the Judith, the Knife, the Milk, the Cheyenne, the White, the Platte, the Kansas, and the Osage.

Marquette and Joliet knew nothing of the geography of that great western river drainage system. But they did believe that in the Missouri River they had found the key to the Northwest Passage. If the waters of the Missouri flowed eastward from some high point of land in the far west of the North American continent down to the Mississippi, they reasoned, then other waters must be flowing westward from the same height of land, down the rest of the way across the continent to empty somewhere into the Pacific Ocean.

The mountains from which the Missouri flowed were thus imagined long before they were seen by Europeans or non-Indian Americans. By the 18th century some geographers were describing these mountains (known at various times as the "Shining" or the "Stony" and, finally, "Rocky" mountains) as representing a "Continental Divide," separating the continent's principal water drainage systems in two. From the Rockies' eastern slopes, it was understood, all waters flowed into the Missouri and the Mississippi River basins, and eventually down to the Gulf of Mexico. From the Rockies' western slopes, all waters must drain to the Pacific.

In 1743, some 70 years after Marquette and Joliet discovered the mouth of the Missouri, Jane Randolph Jefferson gave birth to a son,

This photograph shows the Missouri River, as it can be found now, in a quiet, undisturbed moment. Lewis and Clark hoped that the river would lead them to the Northwest Passage. *(Library of Congress, Prints and Photographs Division [LC-USZ62-309152])*

Thomas, on the family farm in the rural county of Goochland (later Albermarle County), in the British colony of Virginia. Thomas Jefferson's father, Peter Jefferson, a surveyor and mapmaker, owned thousands of acres of good Virginia land. But his hunger for land was unsatisfied. Like many wealthy plantation owners of the era, he was also a land speculator who hoped to profit from the steady westward movement of settlers seeking new lands for farming. In 1749 he was one of the founders of the Loyal Land Company, a partnership speculating in western lands (west, that is, of the Alleghenies, the chain of inland mountains that marked the farthest boundary of settlement for the British colonies).

Peter Jefferson died in 1757 when Thomas, his eldest son, was 14 years old. Thomas inherited his father's property and become a prominent figure among the wealthy elite of plantation owners who ruled 18th century Virginia. But before he did so, he was sent off to study with Reverend James Maury of Fredericksville, Virginia, another Loyal Land Company member, who had a strong interest in geography, an interest he passed on to his student. Shortly before Peter Jefferson died, the Reverend Maury had written a friend describing a plan the Loyal Land Company was devising for a western venture: "Some persons were to be sent in search of that river Missouri . . . in order to discover whether it had any communication with the Pacific Ocean. . . ." Tensions on the frontier, leading in a few years to the outbreak of the French and Indian War, made the plan impractical. Jefferson's father and his friends and associates would never realize their dream of finding a Northwest Passage. That task would be left to the next generation.

A NEW NATION IN THE NEW WORLD

Jefferson's own generation would see the world into which it was born turned upside down. First one empire, and then another, would be thrown down in North America. The French and Indian War of 1754–1763 saw the end of New France, the French empire on the North American continent. All lands east of the Mississippi River, with the exception of Spanish Florida, came under the rule of the British Crown. France lost control of Canada to the British, as well as the long-disputed territory it had claimed in the Ohio valley. And that part of New France known as Louisiana, which stretched northward up the Mississippi River from New Orleans, and westward to the farthest reaches of the Mississippi's watershed, was handed over to Spain.

The collapse of New France meant that the 13 British colonies stretched along the Atlantic seacoast no longer feared attack from the French and their Indian allies. Far from feeling grateful to Great Britain for freeing them from this threat, the colonists began to resent demands from the king and Parliament in faraway London that they should pay taxes to support the continued British military presence in North America.

What happened next is well known, as the colonists' discontent led to colonial rebellion, British retaliation, and finally to the Revolutionary War of 1775–1783 that established national independence. Thomas Jefferson was at the center of these world-shaking events, as representative to the Continental Congress from Virginia, as principal author of the Declaration of Independence adopted by Congress on July 4, 1776, and as wartime governor of Virginia. Following the war, he served the new American nation as congressman, U.S. minister to France, U.S. secretary of state in George Washington's first presidential cabinet, vice president of the United States under John Adams, and finally as the third president of the United States, elected in 1800 and reelected in 1804.

THOMAS JEFFERSON'S SEARCH FOR AN EXPLORER

Jefferson is best remembered for his political achievements, but he once declared that the "tranquil pursuits of science" were his "supreme delight." He sought to increase his own knowledge and the knowledge of his countrymen in fields including agriculture, astronomy, cartography, geography, mathematics, meteorology, and natural history. He was fascinated by American Indians, their customs, and their languages. He was an avid collector of books on scientific and other topics, and the collection he sold to Congress after leaving the White House would form the basis of the Library of Congress. He was also the principal founder of the University of Virginia. The only book he published in his lifetime, *Notes on the State of Virginia,* which appeared in 1787, included a survey of the state's geography, climate, plants, animals, and mineral wealth. Whenever he could— whenever political duties permitted—he devoted himself to his far-ranging scientific interests.

Among the most compelling of those interests was search for the Northwest Passage. It was not a task he could undertake himself; he was not a frontiersman and would, in fact, never venture further west than Harper's Ferry, Virginia (later West Virginia). But he intended to do all he could to encourage others to take up the search. Late in 1783 Jefferson wrote to his friend and fellow Virginian, revolutionary war hero George Rogers Clark, asking if he would be interested in leading an expedition westward to explore the region "from the Mississippi to California." Jefferson was worried that if the Americans did not undertake the exploration of the unknown western half of the continent, the British would, in order to further their ambitions of "colonising into that quarter," as he put it. Clark, who had led American soldiers in the fight against the British and their Indian allies in the Ohio valley, found the prospect of what he described as "a tour to west and North west of the Continent" to be "Extreamly agreable," but had to decline Jefferson's offer. His service in the Revolutionary War had left his finances in disarray, and he could not take the time away from family responsibilities to lead a risky venture such as Jefferson proposed.

Soon afterward, Jefferson sailed to France where he served for five years as ambassador to the United States's most important European ally. But he did not stop thinking of the Northwest Passage. In Paris he met John Ledyard, a native of Connecticut who had been a member of British captain James Cook's famous third expedition exploring the Pacific. In the years between 1776 and 1780 Captain Cook sailed around the tip of Africa to the Indian Ocean, from there to the South Pacific, onward to the Hawaiian Islands, and then to the Pacific Northwest coast of North America.

Cook died before completing the expedition, but Ledyard and others survived to tell the tale. Ledyard published a book in 1783 entitled *A Journal of Captain Cook's Last Voyage to the Pacific Ocean . . . in the Years 1776, 1777, 1778 and 1779*, describing his experiences. Ledyard was probably the first non-Indian American ever to visit the Pacific Northwest, which made him seem an authority on the region. Ledyard's speculations about the

James Cook set an impressive precedent when he explored the Pacific, including the West Coast of North America. Jefferson met with a member of Cook's expedition, John Ledyard; both men had hopes of Ledyard's undertaking an expedition in search of the Northwest Passage. *(Library of Congress, Prints and Photographs Division [LC-USZ62-100822])*

This 1874 steel engraving of Granville Perkins's painting *Harper's Ferry by Moonlight* shows a peaceful aspect at the place where Lewis acquired weapons and an experimental iron boat for the long trip. *(Library of Congress, Prints and Photographs Division [LC-USZ62-051189])*

lucrative possibilities of establishing a Pacific trade route, where sea otter furs gathered in the Pacific Northwest could be traded in China for luxury goods, greatly interested Jefferson, and he was pleased when the explorer sought him out in Paris in 1785. He listened sympathetically while Ledyard described an ambitious plan to find the Northwest Passage.

Ledyard's plan had an interesting twist. Rather than making his way westward up the

heading eastward from Europe, crossing Russia by land, sailing across the Pacific on a Russian trading vessel to the West Coast of North America, and then, somehow, alone and on foot, find his way eastward across the Continental Divide to the Missouri River and eventually all the way to the Mississippi. It was a harebrained scheme, but Jefferson was sufficiently intrigued to provide some financial support for it and tried to secure a passport for the explorer from the Russian government. Little came of the plan. Ledyard set out across Russia in 1788 but was arrested by the Russian authorities before he was halfway across the country and was forced to return to Europe.

Jefferson returned to America in 1789 and took on new duties as U.S. secretary of state. When he was not busy with his official duties, he played a prominent role in the activities of the privately organized American Philosophical Society. Founded by Benjamin Franklin and based in Philadelphia, the American Philosophical Society sought to promote scientific and practical knowledge: Among other projects it hoped to sponsor an expedition to find the Northwest Passage.

André Michaux, a French botanist living in the United States, came to the American Philosophical Society in 1792 with a proposal to lead an expedition for that purpose. Jefferson would probably have preferred an American expedition leader, but he was impressed by Michaux's scientific credentials and undertook fund-raising for the proposed expedition (George Washington was among those contributing). He also wrote out a detailed set of instructions for Michaux in 1793, specifying that "the chief objects of your journey are to find the shortest & most convenient route of communication between the US & the Pacific ocean . . ." Before Michaux could set out up the Missouri, he got mixed up in a shady international

Missouri, the trip Jefferson had encouraged George Rogers Clark to undertake, Ledyard proposed tackling the problem of finding a water route across the continent from another direction altogether. He would set out conspiracy to reestablish French influence in the Louisiana Territory, which brought plans for the expedition to an abrupt halt. The dream of finding the Northwest Passage had run into another dead end. But before the project fell through, an 18-year old U.S. Army officer named Meriwether Lewis had written to Jefferson asking if he could be a member of the expedition. Jefferson, who knew Lewis and his family from Virginia, kept his name in mind for future service.

THE DISCOVERY OF THE COLUMBIA RIVER

In his 1793 letter of instructions to Michaux, Jefferson noted in passing that "the latest maps" suggested that "a river called Oregan interlocked with the Missouri for a considerable distance & entered the Pacific Ocean. . . ." For nearly 30 years, there had been speculation in America and Britain about the existence of a river variously called the "Ouragon," the "Oregan," or the "Oregon," emptying into the Pacific somewhere north of California, with its headwaters in the Rocky Mountains somewhere near those of the Missouri. Robert Rogers, the commander of Roger's Rangers during the French and Indian War, had tried unsuccessfully after the war to interest the British government in sponsoring him on an expedition to discover this river. The existence of an Oregon River was pure hypothesis on the part of explorers and geographers because no white man had ever actually seen, let alone sailed upon it. Captain Cook's exploration of the Pacific Coast had turned up no evidence of its existence.

Where the explorers failed, a private businessman succeeded. In the late 18th century an increasing number of merchant ships were prowling the coast of the Pacific Northwest, trading rum, muskets, beads, and other man-

ufactured goods to the coastal Indian tribes in exchange for furs, especially the highly valued fur of the sea otters found in those waters. As John Ledyard had predicted, there were fortunes to be made carrying the sea otter furs to Chinese ports, where they could be traded for spices, silks, and other luxury goods, which could then be sold for huge profits in London or Boston. In 1792 an American sea captain named Robert Gray, sailing out of Boston to the Pacific Northwest on just such a fur-trading voyage, discovered the mouth of a great river emptying into the Pacific. The Oregon River really did exist, and the dream of finding a Northwest Passage now seemed closer than ever to being realized.

Gray, however, did not call the river by the name Oregon. Instead he named it the Columbia River, after his ship the *Columbia Redivivia*. The discovery of the Columbia by an American gave the United States a somewhat tenuous claim to the Oregon territory. The Stars and Stripes was the first national flag to fly over the Columbia estuary. But Gray was just a private sailor in a merchant ship, acting without any official connection to the U.S. government. Moreover, he generously shared information about the location of the Columbia's mouth with a Royal Navy captain named George Vancouver who was on a mission of exploration in the same region, and it was Vancouver who actually announced Gray's discovery to the world. Vancouver sent one of his subordinates, Lieutenant William Broughton, on an exploratory journey up the river in a longboat. Broughton and his men sailed 100 miles inland, much farther than Gray had gone. At a point of land just past the site of present-day Portland, Oregon, Broughton stepped ashore and declared the surrounding lands to be the possession of the British Crown. Broughton also named some of the most prominent geographical features vis-

Alexander Mackenzie's Expedition across Canada

In 1802 Jefferson read a book entitled *Voyages from Montreal . . . through the Continent of North America, to the Frozen and Pacific Oceans,* published in London in the previous year. Its author was a Scottish-born explorer named Alexander Mackenzie who was an employee of the fur-trading North West Company. *Voyages from Montreal* recorded Mackenzie's journey by canoe and by foot across western Canada to the Pacific Ocean and back in 1792–93.

With a party of nine companions Mackenzie traveled up the Peace River by canoe to the foot of the Rocky Mountains and then crossed the Continental Divide on foot. He made it sound easy—the canoe trip had taken only a month, and he described the pass that led him across the Rockies as "a beaten path leading over a low ridge of land," a mere 3,000 feet in elevation. From there he and his companions made their way to the Pacific Ocean by river part of the way, and then by land. When he reached the ocean, he painted on a cliff face the words "Alexander Mackenzie, from Canada, by land, the twenty-second of July, one thousand seven hundred and ninety three." Although he had not discovered the Northwest Passage, he had crossed the North American continent, the first time it had been done by a non-Indian, and perhaps by anyone. Mackenzie's book outlined a plan for further exploration of the Pacific Northwest, emphasizing the economic importance of establishing British control over the newly discovered Columbia river. "By opening this intercourse between the Atlantic and Pacific Oceans," Mackenzie suggested, "and forming regular establishments throughout the interior . . . as well as along the coasts and islands, the entire command of the fur trade of North America might be obtained." *Voyages from Montreal* proved a wake-up call to Jefferson. If Americans did not act quickly to find their own Northwest Passage, they might well find themselves forever shut out of the Pacific Northwest.

ible from the river, including two of the snow-capped volcanoes of the Cascades range, Mount Hood and Mount St. Helens. Thomas Jefferson was among those who carefully read George Vancouver's 1798 book, *A Voyage of Discovery to the North Pacific,* which included detailed charts of the mouth of the Columbia River and the surrounding lands.

With the long-standing Spanish claim to California, and the new if less well-established British claim to the Oregon territory, the entire

Pacific coast of the North American continent seemed likely to end up as the permanent possession of European colonial powers. Taken together, Spanish and British control of much of the Pacific coast (along with Russian control of Alaska) might well shut U.S. traders out of the increasingly lucrative trade in furs with the coastal Indians. And it would mean that if there were such a thing as a Northwest Passage, its western terminus would be in the hands of a foreign power. At the end of the

18th century, it thus seemed unlikely that the infant republic of the United States, whose westernmost territory then came to an end on the eastern bank of the Mississippi River, would ever become the nation whose lands extended "from sea to shining sea."

PRESIDENT JEFFERSON FINDS HIS EXPLORER

Shortly before his inauguration as third president of the United States in the late winter of 1801, Thomas Jefferson wrote a letter to Meriwether Lewis, the man who eight years earlier had volunteered to go along on the ill-fated American Philosophical Society expedition. Lewis was now 26 years old and a captain in the U.S. Army. "Dear Sir," Jefferson wrote, "The appointment to the Presidency of the U.S. has rendered it necessary for me to have a private secretary." He thought the young army officer would prove the ideal man for the job, even though Lewis had never been to Washington, D.C., or served in any administrative post in the government. "Your knolege of the Western country, of the army and of all it's interests & relations has rendered it desireable for public as well as private purposes that you should be engaged in that office," he wrote. While helping Jefferson with his official correspondence and other matters, Lewis could retain his rank as a captain in the U.S. Army. "Dear Sir," Lewis wrote in reply to the president on March 10, "I most cordially acquiesce, and with pleasure accept the office . . ."

In March 1801 Lewis was veteran of a half-dozen years of uneventful military service in Pennsylvania and Ohio, the U.S. frontier in the 1790s. Born on August 18, 1774, on a plantation called Locust Hill in Albermarle County, Virginia (not far from Monticello), he was the son of William Lewis and Lucy Meriwether

Lewis. Like so many of their countrymen, the Lewis family found its fortunes dramatically changed by the American Revolution, which broke out when Meriwether was a toddler. Shortly after he turned five years old in 1779, his father, a lieutenant in the Continental army, died while returning to the war from a leave to visit his family. Meriwether Lewis did not grow up with any fondness for the British or their colonial ambitions in North America.

Meriwether's mother soon remarried, and for a few years the family lived in Georgia, on some of his stepfather's lands. But the boy was sent back to Locust Hill for schooling at age 13, where he wound up studying with Parson Matthew Maury, the son of Thomas Jefferson's schoolmaster James Maury. Unlike Jefferson's, Lewis's education stopped while he was a teenager. After his stepfather's death his mother and her other children moved back to the family plantation in Virginia. Lewis learned the skills necessary for a Virginia planter: riding, overseeing slaves, and keeping account books. His mother was noted for her skills in herbal medicine, and she may have given him an eye for plants and their uses, which would later prove extremely useful.

Lewis proved to have an adventurous streak that could not be satisfied by the sedentary life of a Virginia planter. In 1795 he enlisted in the Virginia militia and marched off to the frontier to help put down a backwoods rebellion sparked by frontiersmen who resented paying federal taxes (known as the Whiskey Rebellion). It was not much of a rebellion, and all the excitement was over before Lewis got there. But he found that he liked the soldier's life, and transferred to the U.S. Army. The regular standing army was a very small outfit in the 1790s, starved by Congress for men and supplies, and mostly devoted to guarding western settlers against Indian attacks.

As it turned out, Lewis never heard a gun fired in anger over the next six years of frontier duty. In 1801 he was serving as paymaster for the U.S. Army's First Infantry Regiment, whose headquarters were in Pittsburgh. He was a capable officer but may well have wondered about his future; the military being so small and so inactive, there was not much scope for promotion. All things remaining equal, Lewis might well have lived his life out in obscurity, the command of a backwoods military outpost the greatest achievement of his life. Or, worse, he might have been cashiered (dishonorably discharged) from the army for drinking and returned to Virginia in

disgrace because he had a growing for for alcohol that was already getting him into trouble with his superior officers.

All that changed in March 1801 when the letter from Jefferson arrived. As Lewis wrote to a friend and fellow soldier a few days later, "I cannot withhold from you my friend the agreeable intelligence I received on my arrival at this place [Pittsburgh] by way of a very polite note from Thomas Jefferson, the newly elected President of the United States, signifying his wish that I should except [accept] the office of his private Secretary . . ." Lewis confessed that the unexpected offer "did not fail to raise me somewhat in my own estimation,"

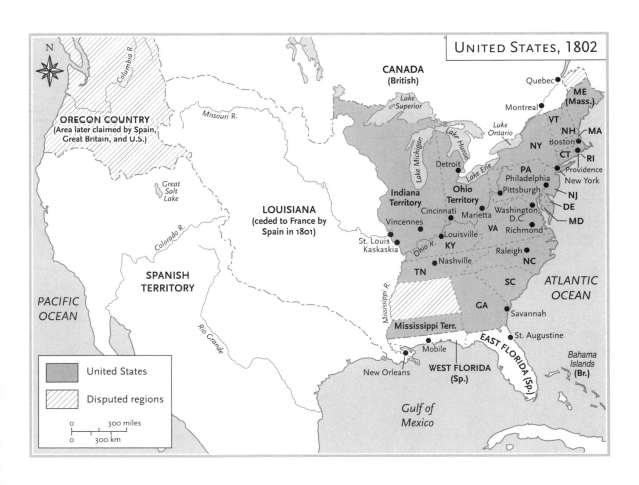

UNITED STATES, 1802

coming as it did from "a man whose virtue and talents I have ever adored . . ." Within the week Lewis was en route to Washington, arriving at the start of April. For the next two years he lived as part of Jefferson's household in the official residence that was then called the President's House and would later be known as the White House. Lewis had a room on the second floor in the east wing of the building; Jefferson lived in the west wing. When Jefferson went home to Monticello for summer vacation, Lewis accompanied him. His tasks, for the most part were routine; he conferred with Jefferson on military and political appointments, carried messages to Congress for the president, and wrote letters on official business. But the company could not have been better.

Despite the difference in their ages (Jefferson was then in his 60s, Lewis in his 20s), the two men grew close. Lewis had lost his father at an early age, and Jefferson had no sons, so it would not be surprising if there was a trace of a father-son bond in their friendship. Nor would it be surprising if, sometime soon after Lewis's arrival in Washington, their conversation turned to the subject of their shared dream of finding the Northwest Passage, though there is no record of just when that topic first arose.

Sometime during those two years they spent in each other's company, most likely in summer or fall 1802, Thomas Jefferson decided that Meriwether Lewis was the man for whom he had long searched to lead an American expedition up the Missouri. Jefferson regretted that the young army officer was not trained as a scientist. Nonetheless, he could see qualities in Lewis that were probably more important to the success of such a daring undertaking than a thorough scientific education, qualities that, as he later wrote, included "firmness of constitution & charac-

ter, prudence, habits adapted to the woods, & a familiarity with the Indian manners and character . . ." Jefferson believed that Lewis had a remarkable gift for "accurate observation" that would allow him to "readily single out whatever presents itself new to him" in the natural world, a habit of mind valuable to both the scientist and the explorer.

In December 1802 Jefferson asked the Spanish minister (or ambassador) in Washington, Carlos Martínez de Yrujo, if his government would have any objection if a small party of American explorers traveled up the Missouri River through the Louisiana Territory, controlled by Spain, on what he described as a purely "literary" (meaning scientific) expedition. Martínez correctly suspected that the U.S. president was not being completely honest about the purposes of the proposed mission. Jefferson, Martínez wrote to his superiors in Madrid, was "a lover of glory" as well as "a man of letters," and probably intended "to discover the way by which the Americans may some day extend their population and their influence up to the coasts of the South Sea [the Pacific]."

Jefferson ignored the unfriendly Spanish response. He would have liked to have secured a Spanish passport for Lewis, but if none was forthcoming the expedition up the Missouri would take place anyway. Having made up his mind that the time was right to realize his long-held dream of finding the Northwest Passage, he acted decisively, if stealthily, to prepare the way for Lewis. On January 18, 1803, he sent a confidential message to the U.S. Congress. "The river Missouri, & the Indians inhabiting it," the president declared, "are not as well known as is rendered desireable by their connection with the Mississippi, & consequently with us." Jefferson proposed a remedy for this problem:

An intelligent officer with ten or twelve chosen men, fit for the enterprize and willing to undertake it, from our posts, where they may be spared without inconvenience, might explore the whole line, even to the Western ocean, have conferences with the natives on the subject of commercial intercourse, get admission among them for our traders as others are admitted, agree on convenient deposits for an interchange of articles, and return with the information acquired in the course of two summers.

In his dealings with Congress, as with the Spanish ambassador, Jefferson was being less than completely honest. His emphasis on the benefits the expedition might yield for American merchants, although certainly a concern of Jefferson's, was not the main purpose of the expedition. He said nothing of the scientific observations that he hoped his "intelligent officer" would carry out en route—he rather doubted whether as president he had the authority under the Constitution to launch an expedition for that purpose. And the possibility that the expedition might find a route all the way to the "Western ocean," was mentioned almost as an afterthought. Any implications such a discovery might have for the expansion of American territory westward to the Pacific were left unspoken. In any case, candid or not, Jefferson's message to Congress produced the results he wished for. In February Congress authorized the expedition, with an appropriation for the sum he asked to pay for it (although the $2,500 that Congress appropriated turned out to be about one-sixteenth of the eventual cost).

The public was not informed of any of this. Jefferson was quietly exultant and let a few close associates from the American Philosophical Society in on the exciting news. "What follows in this letter is strictly confidential," Jefferson wrote in February to Benjamin Smith Barton, professor of botany at the University of Pennsylvania:

> You know we have been many years wishing to have the Missouri explored & whatever river, heading with that, runs into the Western ocean. Congress, in some secret proceedings, have yielded to a proposition I made them for permitting me to have it done: it is to be undertaken immediately, with a party of about ten, & I have appointed Capt. Lewis, my secretary, to conduct it.

3

PREPARING THE WAY
March 1803 to May 1804

In spring 1803 Meriwether Lewis grappled with the daunting question of determining what a dozen or more explorers need to bring with them when crossing thousands of miles of wilderness on river and by foot, across plains, through forests, and over mountains, exposed to summer's heat and winter's cold, uncertain of the route and the reception they might receive from the Native inhabitants.

SEEKING SUPPLIES AND ADVICE

Among the things Lewis and his men certainly were going to need were firearms, both to defend and feed themselves. So in mid-March Lewis left Washington and traveled to the federal arsenal at Harpers Ferry, Virginia. No party traveling west of the Mississippi River had ever carried as impressive a set of weaponry as the rifles that Lewis acquired at Harpers Ferry. These were .54 caliber Model

1803 short rifles, the first the arsenal had ever produced, easier to load and considerably more accurate than the then standard infantry musket. Lewis ordered 15 of the rifles; he should have ordered more, but he had not yet made up his mind just how large an expedition he would lead up the Missouri. (In the end, most of the men carried other weapons; Lewis, for instance, was armed with a long Kentucky rifle, a civilian weapon.)

He also acquired knives, tomahawks, and pistols at Harpers Ferry. And he had a special request for the skilled blacksmiths at the arsenal. He asked them to fabricate an iron frame for an experimental portable boat of Lewis's own design. The entire iron frame for the 30-foot-long vessel could be broken down into 10 sections, each weighing about 22 pounds. If the expedition should come to a difficult portage, either along the Missouri or when it reached the Rockies, and was forced to abandon its boats, he believed that the frame could be lugged overland and down to the next navigable water, then reassembled and covered in animal skins. Lewis believed it would prove a river-worthy craft, capable of carrying up to 8,000 pounds in passengers and supplies. He did not, however, have time to test his theory before ordering the frame to be shipped westward.

In mid-April, Lewis rode on to Lancaster, Pennsylvania. There, Jefferson had arranged for him to be schooled in the art of making celestial observations by the eminent astronomer Andrew Ellicott, another of the president's associates in the American Philosophical Society. Ellicott's lessons would help Lewis plot his location by the position of the stars, establishing a record of longitude and latitude as he moved up the Missouri.

Dr. Benjamin Rush instructed Lewis in basic medicine in preparation for the expedition. *(Library of Congress, Prints and Photographs Division [LC-USZ62-97104])*

Astronomer Andrew Ellicott corresponded frequently with Jefferson and was asked by the president to teach Lewis the art of celestial navigation. *(Library of Congress, Prints and Photographs Division [LC-USZ62-098345])*

In the first week of May Lewis moved on to Philadelphia, where he would spend the next month. He divided his time between meetings with more of Jefferson's scientific friends and securing supplies for the expedition. Lewis would serve as the expedition's doctor as well as its commander, and his Philadelphia mentors included the most famous physician in America, Benjamin Rush. However, most of Rush's advice would prove less than useful where it was not actually harmful to the patients under Lewis's care. It was Rush's considered belief, for example, that powerful laxatives were the first line of defense against disease. While in Philadelphia Lewis stocked up on 600 doses of "bilious pills," or laxatives, for his medical kit. The herbal lore Lewis learned from his mother would, in the actual

Indian Presents

- 5 lb. White Wampum
- 5 lb. White Glass Beads mostly Small
- 20 lb. Red Do. Do. Assorted
- 5 lb. Yellow or Orange Do. Do. Assorted
- 30 Calico Shirts
- 12 Pieces of East India muslin Hanchuchiefs
  Striped or check'd with brilliant Colours.

- 12 Red Silk Hanchuchiefs
- 144 Small cheap looking Glasses
- 100 Burning Glasses
- 4 Vials of Phosforus
- 288 Steels for striking fire
- 144 Small cheap Scizors
- 20 Pair large Do.
- 12 Groce Needles Assorted No. 1 & 8 Common points
- 12 Groce Do. Assorted with points for Sewing leather
- 288 Common brass thimbles — part W. office
- 10 lb. Sewing Thread assorted
- 24 Hanks Sewing Silk
- 8 lb. Red lead
- 2 lb. Vermillion — at War Office
- 288 Knives Small such as are generally used for the Indian trade, with fix'd blades & handles, intaid with brass —

Lewis and Clark left for their mission supplied with an assortment of gifts for potential encounters with Indians. Among these items were trade goods such as ribbon and colored beads. By the time they reached the Pacific, they ran desperately low on these supplies. *(National Archives [NWDTI-92-NM81E225-LEWIS3])* event, prove far more beneficial than the pills that the soldiers on the expedition would come to call "Rush's Thunderbolts." Rush also suggested that in the case of the "least indisposition" on the trail, the explorers should "not attempt to overcome it by labor or marching. Rest in a horizontal position." If that advice had been taken literally, it is doubtful that the expedition would have ever reached the Pacific.

Among the other supplies Lewis purchased in Philadelphia were scientific and navigational instruments, including a chronometer (an accurate clock set to Greenwich Mean Time, necessary for calculating longitude), for which he paid $250. He spent $102.46 on iron goods, $34.15 for copper kettles, $114.42 for shirts, and $25.37 on fishing tackle. From Israel Wheelen, a Philadelphia merchant, he bought 80 "pocket Looking glasses," 72 pieces of striped silk ribbon, and 30-odd pounds of white, yellow, red, and blue beads, all intended as presents or for bartering with the western Indians. By the time Lewis left Philadelphia, he had spent nearly all the money that he and Jefferson had told Congress would be necessary to pay for the entire expedition, and he had yet to purchase any of the boats he would need to carry his men up the Missouri River.

JEFFERSON'S ORDERS

By June 7, Lewis was back in Washington. Over the next few weeks, he and the president doubtless spent many hours together in the White House going over their plans. Jefferson had received advice from his scientific friends in Philadelphia as to the kinds of information Lewis should seek out while on his voyage of discovery. On June 20, Jefferson issued his final instructions for the expedition. "The object of your mission," Jefferson wrote to Lewis,

is to explore the Missouri river, & such principal stream of it, as by it's course and communication with the waters of the Pacific ocean, whether the Columbia, Oregan, Colorado or any other river may offer the most direct & practicable water communication across this continent for the purposes of commerce.

Lewis and Clark's Traveling Library

Tucked in among the tons of food, clothing, ammunition, medical supplies, and trade goods on the keelboat and pirogues, Lewis and Clark carried a traveling library with them on the expedition. Jefferson helped Lewis select a collection of books that might prove useful to the explorers. These included works on botany, mineralogy, astronomy, and medicine. Lewis and Clark also may have carried with them a copy of Alexander Mackenzie's *Voyages from Montreal*, which they made references to in their journals. They even carried a history book, Antoine Le Page du Pratz's *The History of Louisiana, or the Western Parts of Virginia and Carolina*, first published in London in 1763. Lewis had borrowed the book from Dr. Benjamin Smith Barton of Philadelphia in 1803, and returned it to him in 1807, with an inscription noting it had been carried across the continent.

Lewis was to keep careful notations of latitude and longitude of all distinguishing features of the Missouri and Columbia Rivers and the landscape through which the great rivers passed, "especially at the mouths of rivers, at rapids, at islands, & other places & objects distinguished by such natural marks & characters of a durable kind, as that they may with certainty be recognised hereafter." And, most important, he was to employ his new skills in fixing longitude and latitude to determine the location of the "interesting points of the portage between the heads of the Missouri, & of the water offering the best communication with the Pacific ocean. . . ."

Jefferson insisted that Lewis take every possible precaution to ensure that the information he gathered be carefully recorded and preserved. "Several copies of these," Jefferson ordered in reference to Lewis's geographical records, "as well as of your other notes should be made at leisure times & put into the care of the most trustworthy of your attendants . . ."

As for what those "other notes" should include, Jefferson specified that Lewis was to make note of the "names of the [Indian] nations & their numbers" he encountered en route, as well as observations of their relations with other tribes, their languages, their economy, their society, their culture, and their religions.

Nor was that all. Jefferson made a long list of "other objects worthy of notice" for Lewis and the expedition:

> The soil & face of the country, it's growth & vegetable productions, especially those not of the U.S.
> The animals of the country generally, & especially those not known in the U.S.
> The remains or accounts of any which may be deemed rare or extinct;
> The mineral production of every kind. . . .
> Volcanic appearances;

> Climate, as characterised by thermometer, by the proportion of rainy, cloudy, & clear days, by lightning, hail, snow, ice, by the access & recess of frost, by the winds prevailing at different seasons, the dates at which particular plants put forth or lose their flower, or leaf, times of appearance of particular birds, reptiles or insects.

Returning again to the necessity for guaranteeing that a copy of his notes survive, Jefferson urged Lewis to take advantage of any circumstances that would allow him to send back to Washington, perhaps by friendly Indian couriers, or by any merchant ship they might encounter on the Pacific coast, "a copy of your journal, notes & observations of every kind. . . ." This was the only time Jefferson used the word *journal* in his instructions to Lewis, and then only in passing, but it is a word that will always be linked with the expedition. In carrying out President Jefferson's orders, Captain Lewis was required, not only to be an explorer and a military commander, but also a writer. And in this last endeavor, he proved to have gifts that even Jefferson, his intimate companion and great admirer, never suspected. The journals that Lewis kept over the next several years would prove his greatest single legacy to subsequent generations of Americans.

LEWIS FINDS A CO-COMMANDER

President Jefferson closed his list of instructions to Captain Lewis by reminding him of one final duty: "To provide, on the accident of your death, against anarchy, dispersion, & the consequent danger to your party, and total failure of the enterprize, you are hereby authorized . . . to name the person among them who shall succeed to command on your [death]. . . ."

Jefferson and Lewis had, in fact, already agreed on their candidate for second in command. "Dear Clark," Lewis wrote on June 19, 1803: "From the long and uninterupted friendship and confidence which has subsisted between us I feel no hesitation in making to you the following communication under the fulest impression it will be held by you inviolably secret . . ." The man to whom he was writing was a former army officer named William Clark, with whom Lewis had served on the western frontier eight years earlier. Lewis described at some length the mission he had been given to explore the Missouri "as far as it's navigation is practicable," and from there by land to "pass over to the waters of the Columbia or Origan River and by descending it reach the Western Ocean. . . ." Lewis ended with a personal plea to Clark: "If therefore there is anything under those circumstances, in this enterprise, which would induce you to participate with me in it's fatiegues, it's dangers and it's honors, believe me there is no man on earth with whom I should feel equal pleasure in sharing them as with yourself."

Lewis had first met Clark in 1795 at Fort Greenville, Ohio. There he served under Clark's command in an army rifle company for six months. Like Lewis, Clark was a Virginian by birth. He was born August 1, 1770, in Caroline County, Virginia, the ninth child in a family of 10 children. One of his older brothers was George Rogers Clark, a hero of frontier fighting during the American Revolution, and the man who Jefferson had first asked to lead an expedition in search of the Northwest Passage back in 1783. When William was 14, his family moved to a plantation near the Falls of the Ohio in Indiana territory, across the river from present-day Louisville, Kentucky. He

joined the Kentucky militia in 1789 and transferred to the U.S. Army in 1792. Like Lewis, he was an accomplished woodsman, and he was an impressive commanding figure, more than six feet tall. Among his distinguishing features was his hair color; some of the Indians who met him would call him the "Red-Headed Chief." Unlike Lewis, he had actually been involved in fighting the Indians, including the decisive Battle of Fallen Timbers in 1794 that secured the Ohio valley for white settlement. Clark resigned his commission in the army in 1796 to look after family business. Lewis had occasional contact with Clark in the years that followed, but despite the warm words that ended Lewis's letter, they had not been close personal friends.

It took a month for Lewis's letter to reach Clark at his home in Kentucky, and it took him but a day to make up his mind. "Dear Lewis," he wrote on July 18, 1803: "I received by yesterdays Mail, your letter of the 19th . . . The Contents of which I received with much pleasure. . . . This is an undertaking fraited [freighted] with many dificulties, but My friend I do assure you that no man lives whith whome I would perfur to undertake Such a Trip &c. as your self . . ." Lewis had assured Clark that although Lewis would be nominally in command, they would in fact function on the expedition as co-commanders, and that Clark could resume his former army rank of Captain. What had started out as the Lewis expedition was now to be known to posterity as the Lewis and Clark Expedition.

THE LOUISIANA PURCHASE

In his letter inviting Clark to join the expedition, Lewis shared a piece of confidential information then known to only a few people in Thomas Jefferson's administration, namely that "the whole of that immense country wartered [watered] by the Mississippi and it's tributary streams, Missouri inclusive, will be the property of the U. States in less than 12 months from this date. . . ." When Jefferson had first discussed with Lewis the possibility of sending him up the Missouri in search of the Northwest Passage, both men had known that this involved a venture not only into the wilderness but into foreign territory. The moment that Lewis and his party of explorers left the east bank of the Mississippi to cross over to the mouth of the Missouri, they would be leaving U.S. soil. Added to the dangers of the wilderness, and of possibly hostile Indian tribes, Lewis might well find himself challenged and detained by unfriendly Spanish authorities.

The Louisiana Territory, including the city of New Orleans at the mouth of the Mississippi River, had been ceded by France to Spain in 1762, near the end of the French and Indian War. The Spanish were well pleased with the deal because they could use the Louisiana Territory as a buffer zone between their long-established colonies in Mexico and the Southwest, and the British colonies on the Atlantic Coast.

Spain had been the center of Europe's most powerful empire in the 16th and 17th centuries. But by the late 18th century its power was waning in Europe and in the New World. The Spanish flag flew over New Orleans and the little frontier outpost far upriver called St. Louis, but most of the European residents of the territory remained French-speaking. After the American Revolution, land-hungry American settlers were pouring into the Ohio and Mississippi valleys; some were crossing the Mississippi and entering Spanish-controlled territory. Given time, U.S. leaders expected, the Spanish would

inevitably be pushed aside in the Louisiana Territory by the pressure of migrating American settlers.

Expectations that the United States would one day inherit the lands west of the Mississippi were badly shaken by events abroad in 1800–01, when Spain agreed to a proposal from French emperor Napoleon Bonaparte to swap the Louisiana Territory for land he controlled in northern Italy. After a 40-year absence, it looked like France was coming back to North America.

Jefferson was determined to head off the transfer of New Orleans to France. The United States could live with a decaying Spanish empire as a neighbor, but not an aggressive, expansive French empire with a chokehold on the Mississippi. "There is on the globe one spot, the possessor of which is our natural and habitual enemy," Jefferson wrote to American diplomat Robert Livingston in 1802. "It is New Orleans, through which the produce of three-eighths of our territory must pass to market . . ."

Livingston was in Paris, trying to negotiate the purchase of New Orleans from Napoleon's government. Negotiations were not going well. Napoleon planned to send an army of thousands of French soldiers to New Orleans as soon as they finished suppressing a slave rebellion in the French-controlled island of Saint-Domingue (present-day Haiti and the Dominican Republic) in the Caribbean. But the French army on Saint-Domingue met a fateful setback, decimated by yellow fever and by the attacks of the rebellious slaves. Napoleon suddenly decided that he had more pressing business beating the British in Europe, and in spring 1803 ordered his negotiators to offer the Americans not just New Orleans but all of the Louisiana Territory, the entire region of the Missouri watershed that stretched from the Mississippi to the Rocky Mountains. For the bargain price of $15 million, the American

Lewis's Map Collection

Lewis needed to know what to expect in his search for the Northwest Passage. He needed maps. He got one of them from Nicholas King, surveyor for the newly founded city of Washington, D.C. At the request of Albert Gallatin, secretary of the treasury, King prepared a map for Lewis, drawing on the best available knowledge of western geography. The King map gave a fairly accurate representation of the Mississippi River, of the first few hundred miles of the Missouri River, and the Pacific coast around the mouth of the Columbia River. But in between those points, what little detail was given was labeled "conjectural"—which meant it was anybody's guess as to what actually would be found.

Lewis also had a map that Aaron Arrowsmith, a British mapmaker, had published in 1802 and that was advertised as "Exhibiting All the New Discoveries in the Interior Parts of North America." Arrowsmith's map showed Alexander Mackenzie's discoveries in Canada, as well as details of the upper Missouri provided by Hudson's Bay Company fur traders. Like the King map, Arrowsmith depicted the Rocky Mountains as a single and not very impressive mountain range.

When they reached St. Louis, Lewis and Clark were also able to obtain copies of maps drawn by James Mackay and John Evans, who had explored the Missouri as far as villages of the Mandan Indians in the 1790s on behalf of a Spanish-chartered fur-trading company. Although neither Evans or Mackay had traveled west of the Mandan villages, their maps provided useful details about that region, such as the location of the mouth of the Yellowstone River, as well as the location of a great falls along the Missouri. Their maps also suggested that the Rockies might prove a more formidable barrier than the single-ridge line usually depicted.

negotiators in Paris added 565 million acres to the territory of the United States. The Louisiana Purchase brought into U.S. possession the territory that would over the course of the 19th century become the states of Louisiana, Arkansas, Missouri, Iowa, Minnesota, North Dakota, South Dakota, Nebraska, Kansas, Oklahoma, and Montana, as well as about half the future states of Wyoming and Colorado.

Although unofficial reports of the impending sale reached Washington in early June; Jefferson did not receive formal confirmation of the Louisiana Purchase until July 3. Lewis now had the welcome assurance that he would be traveling through U.S. territory until he crossed over the Rockies. On July 5 Lewis left Washington heading westward. Before he left, he wrote a good-bye letter to his mother in Virginia: "[M]y absence will probably be equal to fifteen or eighteen months," he told her. "[T]he nature of this expedition is by no means dangerous. . . . I go with the most perfect preconviction in my own mind of returning safe and hope therefore that you will not suffer yourself to indulge in any anxiety for my safety." Lewis's estimate of the trip's dangers

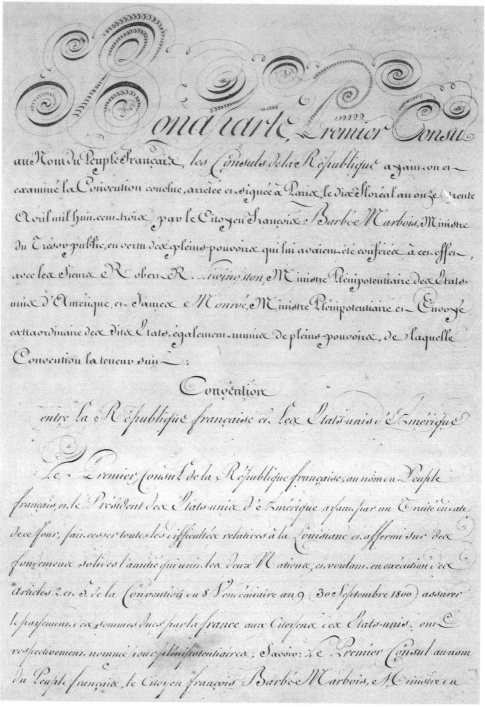

On April 30, 1803, the United States purchased the Louisiana Territory from France, doubling its size. The cost per acre averaged only four cents. Lewis and Clark were the first American citizens to cross the new territory. *(National Archives, Old Military and Civil Records [NWCTB-11-ITAPI159E9-TS(EX)86B])*

France's emperor repossessed the Louisiana Territory from Spain in 1801 only to sell it in its entirety to the United States in 1803. Lewis and Clark were in St. Louis when it passed from French to American possession. (*Library of Congress, Prints and Photographs Division [LC-USZ62-121171]*)

was clearly intended to reassure his mother and may not have reflected his own sober judgment of what he faced in the western wilderness. But his estimate of the trip's duration probably did reflect his thinking in 1803. As it turned out, his estimate was off by nearly a year. It would be two years, five months, and 25 days before he would return to Washington, D.C., to report to President Jefferson.

FROM THE OHIO TO THE MISSISSIPPI

Lewis's first stop after departing Washington was Harpers Ferry, to check on the supplies he had ordered from the federal arsenal. He then rode on to Pittsburgh, where he had contracted with a local boatbuilder to construct a large keelboat. One wagonload of supplies would follow him to Pittsburgh from Harpers Ferry; another was already en route from Philadelphia. Eight soldiers from the fort at Carlisle, Pennsylvania, would also join Lewis in Pittsburgh, to take the keelboat down the Ohio River. They would not accompany the expedition up the Missouri; Lewis was to recruit his expedition members from army posts they would pass while traveling en route to St. Louis.

Lewis arrived in Pittsburgh on July 15. A frontier outpost in the 18th century, Pittsburgh had grown into a city of about 2,400 inhabitants by 1803, a regional transportation hub whose future growth was insured by its location at the junction of the Monongahela and Allegheny Rivers. The city was also becoming a center of American manufacturing, with boatyards and a nail factory.

Lewis looked forward to seeing the keelboat, which according to the assurances he had received from the builder would be ready to launch by July 20. The craft was to be 55 feet long, eight feet wide, with a 32-foot mast, a cabin in the stern, and capable of carrying 10 tons of supplies and a crew of two dozen. It could be propelled by its sails, by 22 oars, by poles, or by towropes, depending on conditions the expedition met along the Missouri.

Lewis was in for a disappointment. The boatbuilder much preferred drink to work, and it would be nearly the end of August before the keelboat was completed. For the next six weeks all Lewis could do was show up at the boatyard and see to it that the builder stayed reasonably sober and attentive to his task. While he waited, he took delivery of the supplies from Harpers Ferry and Philadelphia, and he took command of seven of the eight soldiers who were supposed to accompany him down the Ohio (one deserted before reaching Pittsburgh). Clark's letter accepting his offer of co-command caught up with Lewis while he was in Pittsburgh, which came as welcome news. Lewis also recruited two volunteers, George Shannon and John Colter, who were to become part of the permanent expedition party.

Lewis had originally planned to reach St. Louis by the end of summer and to head up the Missouri some 200 or 300 miles before making winter camp. But fall was coming on, and he still had 1,100 miles to travel by river just to reach the mouth of the Missouri. Finally, on August 31, Lewis and his crew of 10 or possibly 11 men (the seven soldiers, two or

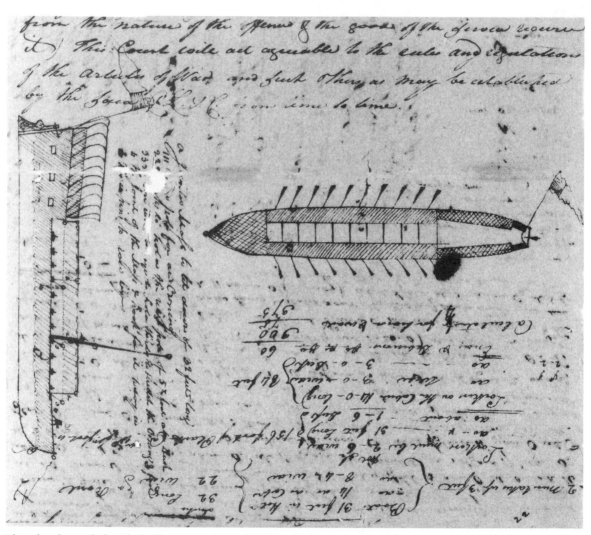

This sketch, made by Clark, illustrates the 55-foot-long keelboat designed by Lewis and modified by Clark. *(Yale Collection of Western Americana, Beinecke Rare Book and Manuscript Library)*

possibly three new recruits, and a pilot who was to help them navigate the Falls of the Ohio) set off down the Ohio River. Seaman, a black Newfoundland dog that Lewis had bought for company in Pittsburgh for $20, accompanied them. There were now two boats in Lewis's little fleet: the keelboat and a pirogue that he also purchased in Pittsburgh (the *pirogue,* as Lewis used the term, was a flat-bottomed open boat that could be rowed or rigged with a sail).

Because of the shallow water in late summer, Lewis did not want to overload the boats. Some of the expedition supplies were sent overland by wagon to Wheeling, Virginia (now West Virginia), where the river deepened. Even with the lightened load, the men frequently had to get out, unload and portage the cargo downriver, and then drag the boats through shallow places in the river. They had other troubles as well, further slowing their progress. Rain was rusting their rifles, tomahawks, and knives and spoiling the supply of biscuits, forcing them to halt to dry their goods and repackage them. The pirogue Lewis acquired in Pittsburgh leaked, as did a replacement craft he picked up en route a few days later. In Wheeling on September 9 Lewis purchased a larger pirogue that served them better. It is difficult to keep track of the expedition's boats, but somewhere along the way en route to the Mississippi that fall, Lewis seems to have acquired both the red and the white pirogue that would carry his men up the Missouri.

Lewis was already keeping his eyes open for interesting natural phenomena that he could report to Jefferson. On September 11 he saw something that astonished him: a large number of grey squirrels swimming "light on the water" across the Ohio River. He was at a loss to explain the mass migration, since both sides of the river were equally well supplied

with nut-bearing trees. Lewis's interests in the swimming squirrels as a naturalist soon gave way to another interest: satisfying his appetite. He sent Seaman the Newfoundland dog into the river to kill some of the squirrels and fetch them back to the boat. "[T]hey wer fat," Lewis wrote contentedly in the journal he was starting to keep, "and I thought them when fryed a pleasant food." Two days later, the squirrels were still to be seen crossing the river. He also mentioned seeing a flock of passenger pigeons flying southward—something that did not surprise him, because passenger pigeons, extinct by the beginning of the 20th century, were known in Lewis's time for passing overhead in such huge numbers that they darkened the skies.

Lewis stopped writing in his journal on September 18; the first of many gaps in his journal-keeping on the expedition; he would resume writing in it on November 11; but only for two weeks. Why Lewis chose to disregard Jefferson's instructions about record-keeping for long periods between 1803 and 1806 remains one of the unresolved mysteries of the expedition.

In the meantime, he continued his progress down the Ohio. Stopping in Cincinnati on September 28, Lewis took some time off from the journey to explore a local site known for its fossil remains. Lewis may have decided the delay was worthwhile because he knew how much Jefferson was fascinated by the science of paleontology. He packed up a box of bones, including some that he thought were remains of wooly mammoths, and shipped them back to Washington (they were lost en route, to Jefferson's disappointment).

On October 14, a month and a half after setting off from Pittsburgh, Lewis and his men reached Clarksville, in Indiana Territory, where William Clark lived with his older and ailing brother George Rogers Clark. The expe-

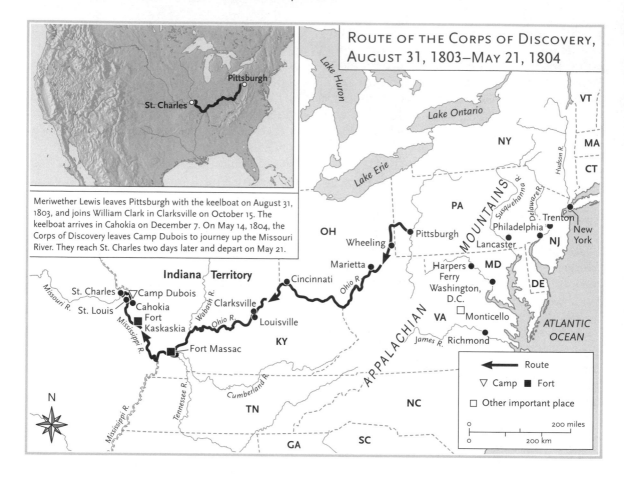

ROUTE OF THE CORPS OF DISCOVERY,
AUGUST 31, 1803–MAY 21, 1804

Meriwether Lewis leaves Pittsburgh with the keelboat on August 31, 1803, and joins William Clark in Clarksville on October 15. The keelboat arrives in Cahokia on December 7. On May 14, 1804, the Corps of Discovery leaves Camp Dubois to journey up the Missouri River. They reach St. Charles two days later and depart on May 21.

dition was now beginning to take shape. At Lewis's request, Clark had been busy lining up recruits, and he introduced Lewis to seven young volunteers from Kentucky: William Bratton, George Gibson, John Shields, Charles Floyd, Nathaniel Pryor, and brothers Reuben and Joseph Field. They were sworn into the army along with Shannon and Colter. By the standards of the U.S. military in the early 19th century, these men were to be well compensated for their service. To attract qualified recruits, Lewis secured double pay for the men on the expedition ($10 a month for enlisted men, instead of the standard $5), plus the promise of early discharge on their return,

and a western land bounty of several hundred acres for each man who went along. One man who joined the expedition at Clarksville would not be paid anything at all, however: That was York, an African-American slave owned by William Clark. York was a powerful, heavyset man with "short curling hair" about Clark's age, who had been his companion since childhood.

On October 26, after spending two weeks resting and refitting in Clarksville, Lewis and Clark and their men set off down the Ohio, passing through present-day Illinois. On November 11 they reached Fort Massac, an old French fortification located on a commanding promontory above the Ohio that had been restored by the Americans. There they added two new recruits to the expedition's roster, John Newman and Joseph Whitehouse, plus a civilian, George Drouillard (in their journal entries, the captains would refer to him as "Drewyer"). Drouillard brought valuable skills to the expedition, including his ability to interpret the sign language that allowed Indians of many different tribes and spoken languages to communicate among themselves. He was also a first-rate hunter and trail finder. He would prove well worth the $25 a month he was paid for his services. Among Lewis's qualities as a leader was the fact that he was a good judge of men and could quickly size up who should be entrusted with important tasks. He immediately dispatched Drouillard on a mission to another army post, South West Point, Tennessee, to find eight soldiers who were waiting there to join the expedition. When they finally caught up with the expedition five weeks later, Lewis rejected four of the men as unfit for wilderness travel.

From Fort Massac, the expedition sailed down the Ohio to its junction with the Mississippi River, near present-day Cairo, Illinois. They spent six days there, while Lewis and Clark familiarized themselves with their navigational instruments and practiced the vital task of determining longitude and latitude. On November 20 they set off northward up the Mississippi, the river that the Algonquian Indians called "the Father of Waters" and that drains the water from 40 percent of the continental United States. Although the Mississippi's course was well known by this point, Clark began to record the river's twists and turns, with compass bearings, perhaps practicing the record-keeping he would need to keep along the Missouri.

As they headed northward, they were traveling between the separate countries. The Illinois Territory, part of the United States, formed the east bank of the river, the Louisiana Territory, which was still officially governed by the Spanish, and not scheduled to be handed over to the United States until the following spring, lay to the west. After two days, they passed by a U.S. settlement on the Spanish side of the river where 15 American families were already established, the advance guard of thousands who would soon be pouring into the territory. They also passed keelboats heading up the river with dry goods and whiskey to sell to American settlers on the Illinois side, and other keelboats heading down to New Orleans loaded with furs. They reached the U.S. Army military post Fort Kaskaskia on the Illinois side of the river, on November 28, where they added at least six more volunteers to the expedition's strength.

THE EXPEDITION'S FIRST WINTER

Winter was coming on, and they would soon need to make a permanent encampment for its duration. At Fort Kaskaskia, Lewis and Clark split up. Lewis borrowed a horse and rode north along the Illinois side of the river, arriving at the American settlement at Cahokia, across the river from St. Louis, on December 7. He crossed the river to the city the following day. In 1803 St. Louis was celebrating the 40th year since its founding. It was still a very small community of about 1,000 residents huddled along the banks of the Missouri.

On December 8, Lewis met with the Spanish governor of the city, Colonel Carlos Dehault Delassus. Colonel Delassus was not overly welcoming. He had as yet received no official notification of the Louisiana Purchase, and he reminded Lewis that as an American he was still a guest on foreign territory. And he made it clear that Lewis could not begin his exploration of the Missouri that winter—a plan that the captains had already abandoned in any case.

Lewis received a friendlier reception from the city's wealthy fur-trading merchants, including Manuel Lisa and half-brothers Auguste and Pierre Chouteau. The merchants knew that their own economic futures were bound up now with the westward expansion of the United States, and they were eager to ingratiate themselves with the new rulers of the Louisiana Territory, as well as to sell the American captain the goods he would need to outfit his ever-expanding expeditionary force. They proved useful sources of information on both the geography and the Indians of the Missouri, at least along its first few hundred miles as it stretched westward from St. Louis. Antoine Soulard, a Frenchman employed by the Spanish governor as surveyor-general for Upper Louisiana, provided

Lewis with a copy of a map he had drawn, showing in detail the course of the Missouri up to the Mandan villages, and offering a speculative depiction of what lay further west.

While Lewis was attending to business in St. Louis, Clark led the rest of the expedition up the river, past St. Louis to the mouth of the Wood River. Here they would make their winter camp, at a site directly across the Mississippi from the mouth of the Missouri. What is known of the winter at Camp Wood (a name given the site by historians of the expedition, not one used by Lewis and Clark themselves) comes almost entirely from Clark's journal. Lewis's silence as a writer would last, with brief exceptions, until April 1805. Clark was now the principal day-to-day recorder of the expedition's fortunes and progress. He tended to be terse and matter-of-fact at first, providing few details beyond the orders he gave the men and the weather. Thus the entry for December 13 read, in its entirety:

St. Louis
GATEWAY TO THE WEST

Had France not lost its war with Britain and the American colonies, St. Louis could have cemented French power on the Mississippi and the Missouri. But the little village community with its prime strategic location passed under the control of the Spanish authorities, who neglected its potential. Instead it was left to the Americans, along with some well-established French traders like René Auguste Chouteau and his half-brother Jean-Pierre Chouteau, to fully realize St. Louis's importance as "Gateway to the West."

The American writer Washington Irving visited the city soon after the Louisiana Purchase, and he described it in the moment of transition: "Here and there were new rich houses and ships, just set up by bustling, driving, and eager men of traffic from the Atlantic states; while, on the other hand, the old French mansions, with open casements, still retained the easy, indolent air of the original colonists."

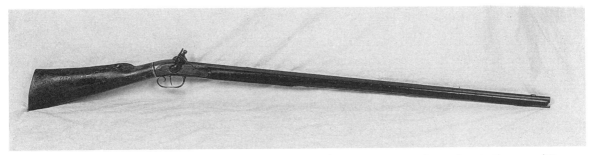

Captain Lewis bought an air gun at Harper's Ferry in 1803 at his own expense. According to the expedition journals, the firing of the air gun never failed to "astonish" Native American viewers. Lewis hoped that this display of technological prowess would make the Indian tribes all the more willing to trade with white Americans in the future. *(VMI Museum, Lexington, VA)*

fixed on a place to build huts Set the men to Clearing land & Cutting logs—a hard wind all day—flying Clouds, Sent to the neghbourhood, Some Indians pass.

It snowed on December 15. By December 22, Clark was recording that the Mississippi was "[C]overd with running Ice." At Christmas, they were finishing up their winter huts. "[T]he men frolicked and hunted all day," Clark noted, coming back with several turkeys shot in the neighboring woods for Christmas dinner. But some of them went overboard in their celebration. Clark recorded, "Some of the party had got Drunk (2 fought.)" The drinking and the brawling were indications of the poor morale and boredom often to be found in an army winter camp. There was not enough for the men to do, and they seemed to feel little in the way of loyalty to each other or to their leaders. On New Year's Day Clark sponsored a shooting contest between the soldiers and some local men who had come to the camp to visit, offering a dollar to the winner (the soldiers lost to the civilians); there was also more drunkenness in the camp. Three days later there was another fight in the camp; the men "bruse

themselves much," Clark complained in his journal.

Gradually, Clark's journal-keeping grew more inventive and interesting. In addition to the record of turkeys shot and fights between the men, Clark began to insert sketches in his notebook, including a several of the keelboat and one of the white pirogue. (Both Clark and Lewis turned out to have a gift for line drawings, which greatly enrich the stock of visual images of the expedition.) When the men finished building the huts, Clark put them to work improving the keelboat. Modifications included the building of storage lockers along the sides, which came equipped with heavy wooden lids that could be raised to provide protection for men in the boat in case of attack. They also mounted a swivel gun, a small cannon that could fire either a small cannonball or a load of musketballs, on the bow of the keelboat, and two blunderbusses, heavy, shotgunlike weapons with a bell-shaped mouth, mounted at its stern. Each of the two pirogues the expedition would take up the Missouri also had a blunderbuss mounted on its stern.

After a long absence in St. Louis and Cahokia, Lewis briefly rejoined the expedition in February. Clark got a welcome chance to cross the river to St. Louis and enjoy a little of its social life. (Camp life had not agreed with Clark that winter; "I was unwell" was a recurring entry in Clark's journal throughout January and early February.) Lewis spent only a few days at Camp Wood. For most of February both captains were in St. Louis, leaving Sergeant John Ordway in command. The captains' prolonged absences did not help the camp's disciplinary problems. The men may have resented the fact that their officers were getting to spend the winter enjoying the comforts of St. Louis, while they were stuck out in the woods, in freezing temperatures, with nothing to look forward to beyond their evening ration of whiskey. At times it seemed as if mutiny threatened the success of the expedition. Reuben Field refused to take his turn at guard duty, and other soldiers loudly and belligerently took his side. John Shields and John Colter defied Ordway's orders and threatened to kill him. Lewis could be a strict disciplinarian, but he decided not to discharge the troublemakers (possibly because there were too many of them). As things turned out, some of the worst offenders that winter proved to be among the most devoted and competent soldiers once the expedition set off up the Missouri.

"WE PROCEEDED ON . . ."

On March 10, 1804, the Stars and Stripes was raised over St. Louis. Lewis was there as the official representative of the U.S. government for the ceremony that saw the Louisiana Territory handed over, first from Spain to France, and then from France to the United States. They were no longer on foreign soil when they stood on the west bank of the Mississippi.

That was certainly good news. So was the arrival of spring shortly thereafter. By March

20 frogs could be heard croaking, by March 26 Clark was recording the weather as "worm and fair," by April 1 the spicewood was in bloom, followed soon after by apple and peach trees, and by the noisy passage of flocks of waterfowl flying northward. Lewis and Clark planned to get an early start up the Missouri. Clark calculated that they would travel 1,500 miles to reach the Mandan villages, the last well-described location on their maps. His calculations were only about 100 miles short of the actual distance. He further calculated that it would be 1,550 miles from the Mandan villages to the Pacific Ocean. There he erred significantly; his calculations were 1,000 miles too short. Making 10 or 12 miles a day, Clark figured the expedition should be able to travel as far as the headwaters of the Missouri in the Rocky Mountains by September 1804, and then push on the following spring to reach the Pacific in summer 1805.

Departure was set for April 18. With the help of the Chouteau brothers, the expedition hired seven French boatmen, known as *engagés*, who had experience sailing up the Missouri as far as the Mandan villages. But in the end, they were delayed. Lewis needed more time to lay in last-minute supplies, and he also had to make complicated arrangements for Pierre Chouteau to lead a delegation of Osage Indians to Washington, D.C., to meet their new "great white father," Thomas Jefferson.

By the time everything was sorted out, necessary supplies gathered and packed in the expedition's three boats, it was mid-May. Meanwhile, Clark had received disappointing news from Washington. Despite Lewis's promise that Clark would hold rank equal to his own, Jefferson had secured him a commission only as a lieutenant. Clark was angry, and Lewis sympathized completely. The two officers agreed they would make no mention of the difference in rank to their men, and throughout the expedition Lewis referred to Clark as "Captain Clark," as most historians have done ever since.

There was more last-minute packing to do. Clark took the loaded keelboat out onto the Mississippi on a test cruise. The men were issued ammunition for their weapons: 100 rounds each for the men carrying rifles, two pounds of buckshot for the men carrying muskets. Finally, on May 14, 1804, it was time to go. Lewis was in St. Louis, still tending to the Osage delegation. He would join the expedition after a few days. Clark was in command of the keelboat and the two pirogues, and on the evening of May 14 he wrote in his journal: "I set out at 4 oClock P.M. in the presence of many neighboring inhabitents, and proceeded on under a jentle brease up the Missouri. . . ."

4

UP THE MISSOURI
May to October 1804

Sometime toward the end of their stay at Camp Wood, William Clark wrote a note to himself calculating the number of men in "our party." His list included: "2 Capts. 4 Sergeants, 3 Intptrs. [Interpreters], 22 Amns [Americans]. 9 or 10 French, & York also 1 Corpl. & Six in a perogue. . . ." One of the "Capts," Meriwether Lewis, was in St. Louis, so he was not on board with the rest of the men when they set sail up the Missouri on May 14. "Intptr" George Drouillard was also away on an errand, and the other two interpreters on Clark's list may have been men who had arranged to join the expedition a few days later.

Lewis, Clark, the three sergeants—Ordway, Floyd, and Pryor (Clark's "4 Sergeants" seems to have been a slip of the pen)—along with the 22 "Amns" (Americans), the three interpreters, and Clark's black servant York—31 men all told—constituted the expedition's permanent party, the men who were intended to go all the way to the Pacific and back. They would travel on the keelboat. The "9 or 10 French" (a later list of Clark's would account for only eight) were the engagés, the hired boatmen, who would accompany the expedition only as far as the Mandan villages. They traveled in the 41-foot-long red pirogue. And the "Corpl. and Six in a perogue" were Corporal Richard Warfington and his detachment (a later list by Clark would account for only five men serving under Warfington), who were to travel some distance up the Missouri with the permanent party but to return before winter set in to St. Louis. They were assigned the smallest vessel, the 35-foot-long white pirogue. Clark's somewhat undependable count of expedition members has led historians to varying conclusions as to just how many men actually set sail on May 14, with estimates ranging between 43 and 48.

LAST CONTACTS WITH WHITE SETTLEMENTS

Departing in the late afternoon, the men of what Jefferson had dubbed the "Corps of Discovery" made modest progress that first day.

They crossed the Mississippi and pushed a short way up the Missouri. They camped that night by a small creek near Fort Belle Fontaine, in present-day North St. Louis. The men probably missed their snug cabins at Camp Wood, as it rained so steadily they could not keep their campfires burning. These first days of travel were useful as a shakedown cruise. Some of the cargo was getting wet beneath its covers. The keelboat was having problems on the river, snagging on floating logs, and riding too high at its bow; some of the goods stowed in the stern of the boat would have to be moved forward to balance the load. One of the other vessels, probably the white pirogue with Corporal Warfington's detachment, was, as Clark noted, "not Sufficiently maned [manned] to Keep up."

On May 16 they reached the little village of St. Charles, located on the north bank of the river, about 21 miles upriver from the mouth of the Missouri. With its 450 inhabitants, St. Charles was the last substantial white settlement they would encounter until their return. Clark and the men spent five days there, waiting for Lewis to finish his business in St. Louis and join them. It was their last chance to enjoy some familiar pleasures: Private Joseph Whitehouse reported in the journal he was beginning to keep that it was "verry agreeable dancing with the french ladies, &c."

It was not all play. Clark had the men reload the keelboat and one of the pirogues and pack in some last-minute supplies (including an additional 136 pounds of tobacco). Clark had to convene a court-martial for three expedition members who committed various offenses in St. Charles; one of them, John Collins, was accused of behaving in an "unbecomeing manner" at a dance as well as "Speaking in a language . . . tending to bring into disrespect the orders of the Commanding officer," infractions that earned him a sentence of 50 lashes on his bare back.

Two new members joined the expedition at St. Charles, although they may have been recruited earlier. One was Pierre Cruzatte, who would play a prominent role in many of the events to follow. Half French and half Indian, he was an experienced boatman. Although blind in one eye and able to see none too well out of the other, he would usually take up the important position of bowman on the keelboat, guiding the boat through the many hidden dangers the river held. He was also valued by other expedition members for his skill in playing the fiddle. The other new recruit was François Labiche, also half French and half Indian, who would serve

Although Lewis and Clark passed the settlement to which Daniel Boone had moved in 1799, they did not meet Boone. *(Library of Congress, Prints and Photographs Division [LC-USZ62-112549])*

the expedition as a translator in addition to his regular duties.

Lewis rejoined the party on May 20, and the following day, at half past three, the expedition pushed off up the Missouri. Once more they "procceded on under a jentle Breese"—at least for a mile, until they found themselves engulfed in "a Violent rain with Wind from the S.W. . . ." Over the next few days they passed a few small farms scattered along the riverside, including the settlement in present-day St. Charles County, Missouri, where Daniel Boone, the legendary American frontiersman, had moved in 1799. On May 25 the expedition came to the last white settlement along the Missouri, La Charrette, near present-day Marthasville, Missouri. Seven families lived there, who depended on trade with the Indians for their livelihood. They obtained corn and eggs from the local inhabitants, and according to Clark also obtained "a good Deel of information" about upstream Indian tribes from French trader Regis Loisel.

Even these first days of travel, still so close to white settlements, were not without their dangers. In fact, the expedition might have come to an abrupt end on May 23, when Lewis decided to explore the edge of a rocky embankment towering some 300 feet above the Missouri. He lost his footing at its very top and slid 20 feet downward before catching himself by jamming his knife into a crack in the rock. A few more feet and he would have gone tumbling down to the rocks and water below, and the Corps of Discovery, if it "proceeded on" after losing its leader, would not have gone down in history as the Lewis and Clark Expedition. Thomas Jefferson once said of Captain Lewis that he was the possessor of "courage undaunted," which was certainly true. But his courage occasionally shaded off into a darker quality in his character. Though

he kept it in check much of the time, Meriwether Lewis had a reckless streak.

SETTLING INTO ROUTINE

The Corps of Discovery averaged about 15 miles a day on the Missouri that summer. Each day Clark noted in his journal the direction the river traveled through its many twists and turns, and the distance covered. Clark tended to underestimate distances traveled by river, and overestimate distances traveled by land, but on the whole the records left in the journals proved remarkably accurate when rechecked by geographers and historians in later years.

The men were usually up at first light, about 5 A.M. They would eat a hasty breakfast, strike their tents, and be on the river soon after. On most days that they were traveling, Clark would stay with the boats, while Lewis usually roamed the shore on foot. Sometimes they got lucky and their sails could propel them upstream: "The wind favourable today," Clark noted happily on May 26, "we made 18 miles." Sometimes a back eddy in the river's current would carry them upstream, while the men rested from their efforts. But usually their progress came at the expense of hard human labor: rowing, poling, or even getting out and pulling the boats upstream with towropes, while the Missouri's fast-flowing waters tried to sweep them back down the river to St. Louis. After a day's travel, they would halt, by a convenient creek if they could find one, unload the goods they needed for the night, pitch their tents, and prepare the one hot meal they would enjoy during the day.

Game was abundant, and they ate heartily, consuming as much as eight or nine pounds a day per man. The deer steaks, antelope steaks, buffalo steaks, or whatever meat the hunters happened to bring in the day would

Charles M. Russell's work *Nature's Cattle* (1899) is of antelope and buffalo grazing, two animals that the Corps of Discovery depended on for nourishment and hides. *(Library of Congress, Prints and Photographs Division [LC-USZ62-115203])*

be supplemented by grapes, plums, berries, and greens picked along the way, flat bread made from cornmeal or flour, and salt pork if the hunters were not successful. For his 34th birthday, on August 1 Clark ordered a special meal to be prepared, consisting of "a Saddle of fat Vennison, an Elk fleece & a Bevertail to be cooked and a Desert of Cheries, Plumbs, Raspberries Currents and grapes of a Supr. [superior] quallity." Some nights the captains would issue each man a four-ounce ration of whiskey and, despite their weariness, the men would celebrate with dancing while Cruzatte played his fiddle. On the Fourth of July in 1804, which they celebrated in present-day Atchison County, Kansas, near the mouth of the Kansas River, they marked the occasion not only with whiskey but also with cannon fire. Generally, however, the evenings were times of quiet relaxation and early bedtimes. Everyone knew that another day's hard labor awaited them when the Sun rose in the morning.

Lewis and Clark had carefully selected the men who made up the Corps of Discovery, weeding out those who they felt might not be up to the rigors of wilderness travel. But within a month or so after St. Louis, many of the men were feeling the worse for wear. The aches and pains of hard physical labor were made worse by the unremitting assault of stinging insects. Lewis had had the foresight to include mosquito netting in the expedition's supplies, and the men smeared grease over their exposed skin to keep off bloodsucking pests, but such preventive measures were only partially successful. "The Ticks & Musquiters are verry troublesome," Clark reported on June 17, in what became a constant refrain in his journal. Other ailments added to the misery of aches, pains, and mosquito bites, with many suffering from boils on their skin or stomach troubles. Clark in his journal attributed such ills to drinking the river water, but they were probably the product of badly preserved meat and too few fruits and vegetables in their diet. Clark had difficulty shaking a bad cold and sore throat he developed in mid-June.

The worst medical crisis the expedition would face came in late summer. Sergeant Charles Floyd had not been feeling well for several weeks. Then on August 19, Clark noted in his journal that "Serjean Floyd is taken verry bad all at once with a Biliose Chorlick [a 'bilious colic,' a term then used to describe malaria]." Clark stayed up most of that night with Floyd, ministering to him as best he could (probably with some of Dr. Rush's laxatives). The following day, he had sad news to record in his journal: "Sgt. Floyd died with a great deal of composure; before his death he Said to me, 'I am going away. I want you to write me a letter.'" Floyd's "bilious colic" was in all likelihood a ruptured appendix, a condition that was untreatable in the early 19th century, even by skilled doctors. Floyd, a native of Kentucky, was among the first to join the Corps of Discovery and was, in Clark's estimate, "[a] man of much merit." He was just 22 years old when he died. He was buried with full military honors on a hill overlooking the Missouri River in present-day Sioux City, Iowa. The men called it "Floyd's Bluff," the name by which it is still known. Private Patrick Gass was elected by the men to take Floyd's place as a sergeant.

The disciplinary problems that had plagued the expedition in winter camp were still evident those first months on the river. The way that Lewis and Clark dealt with such problems serves as a reminder that the Corps of Discovery was a military unit moving through hostile territory and not a group of friends out on an extended camping trip. On June 29, the captains convened a court-martial to hear the case of Privates John Collins and Hugh Hall, accused of tapping the expedition's whiskey barrel the night before, with the result that Collins was drunk while on guard. The court was made up of Sergeant Pryor and five enlisted men. Collins, who had behaved badly at St. Charles just six weeks earlier, was sentenced to 100 lashes, while Hall got 50 lashes. The entire party assembled at 3 P.M. to watch the sentence carried out. The beaten men had to go right back to work, with their bloody backs, rowing, poling, and hauling the keelboat upstream. It was a harsh punishment, but one that must have seemed just to the rest of the Corps of Discovery: A drunken guard endangered all their lives. They also knew that there was going to be no tavern along the next several thousand miles where they would be able to replenish their supply of whiskey when it ran out; Collins and Hall had enjoyed themselves at the expense of their fellow expedition members.

Private Alexander Willard faced a court-martial July 12 after Sergeant Ordway had discovered him lying asleep while on guard duty the previous night. The accusation against Willard was so serious that, unlike previous courts, made up of enlisted men, Lewis and Clark themselves served as the court; under the military's Articles of War, Willard could have been sentenced to death by firing squad. The two captains found Willard guilty as charged and sentenced him to 100 lashes on his bare back. Private Moses Reed deserted on August 4. He had told the captains he had left a knife behind at the previous night's campsite and would go and fetch it and then return. When he had not returned four days later, the captains sent out a party consisting of Drouillard and three other men to find Reed and bring him back dead or alive. He was brought in alive on August 17, sentenced to run the gauntlet four times (which meant being beaten with willow switches by the entire party), and removed from the permanent party in disgrace. (Private Robert Frazer, part of Corporal Warfington's detachment, later signed on as a member of the permanent party, to replace Reed.) One of the engagés also deserted but was never caught. Finally, Private John Newman was court-martialed on October 13 for statements "of a highly criminal and mutinous nature," found guilty, and sentenced to 75 lashes and dishonorable discharge from the army and the expedition (though he, like Moses Reed, would, of necessity, accompany them to the winter encampment).

THE GREAT PLAINS

Every few days, Lewis and Clark noted something that was new to them. In June they began to see white pelicans along the river. Clark killed one in August, and as an experiment he had his men fill its bill and neck pouch with water; it held five gallons.

The landscape was no less strange than the wildlife. Whether they had grown up in Virginia, like Lewis and Clark, in Kentucky, like Sergeant Floyd, or in New Hampshire, like Sergeant John Ordway, the men of the Corps of Discovery were most familiar with hilly or even mountainous landscapes covered with dense forests. Where there was open land, it was land that had been cleared, either by Indians or white settlers. Since leaving Camp Wood in May, however, the Corps of Discovery had entered a region of grasslands, very different than the landscape they knew at home. This was an open country, level or with low rolling hills, with views that stretched for miles, and the openness was not the product of human design.

Still, there were similarities with the world they had left behind. Both the wooded hills of Virginia and New England and the prairie

After seeing what seemed to them acres covered by flocks of pelicans, Lewis and Clark named the island where they saw the massive amounts of birds Pelican Island. *(Library of Congress, Prints and Photographs Division [LC-USZ62-95232])*

grasslands of Missouri were the recipients of regular rainfall. There were tall, luxuriant grasses on the prairie, and both the river bottoms and the bluffs along the river were often heavily wooded with cottonwoods, sycamore, and hickory trees, as well as an underbrush of grapevines and rushes. The Corps of Discovery could easily imagine farmers and their livestock following in their wake. Writing on July 4, Clark noted that "[t]he Plains of this

According to Lewis's journal, the Great Plains were covered by herds of game in 1804. By 1870, when this photograph was taken, overhunting by settlers, railroad workers, and game hunters had greatly diminished the source of food. *(National Archives [NWDNS-57-HS-348])*

The "Barking Squiril"

The strangeness of the animal population on the Great Plains added to the explorers' sense of wonder as they encountered this new landscape. On September 7, Lewis and Clark came across a burrowing animal unlike any they had ever seen before. It lived in what Clark described as a "village" containing "great numbers of holes on the top of which those little animals Set erect . . ." When Lewis and Clark approached them, they made "a Whistleing noise" before slipping into their holes. Lewis called this creature a "barking squiril," but it was Sergeant John Ordway who came up with the name for them that would catch on: *prairie dogs*. The Corps of Discovery spent the better part of the day trying to capture one by flushing out its burrow with kettles of water. They finally succeeded, and the "barking squiril" miraculously survived and was sent east to be viewed by Thomas Jefferson in the White House a year later.

This black-tailed prairie dog was unfamiliar to the Corps of Discovery when the men first encountered it. John Ordway gave the burrowing animal the name by which it is known today. *(U.S. Fish and Wildlife Service)*

country are covered with a Leek green Grass, well calculated for the sweetest and most nourishing hay . . ."

Americans were used to thinking of land in this way—a fertile, bountiful resource waiting to be dug up and planted, a Garden of Eden in a Promised Land. But the landscape changed dramatically when they passed north of the mouth of the Platte River in late July and moved into the semiarid region of the Great Plains. The tall grass of the central lowland of the lower Missouri gave way to short grass of the upper Missouri. Trees grew scarcer, apart from the cottonwoods that still sprang up along the river bottoms. Strong winds blew across the treeless plains, with nothing to break their force. The alkaline soil left a white powdery deposit on its surface and gave a bitter taste to the water flowing down the creeks into the Missouri.

The farmers in the Corps of Discovery may have looked out over the Great Plains and shaken their heads doubtfully. But for the hunters, the region was still a land of bounty. In the woodlands of the east a herd of deer or other game animals might consist of a dozen or so members. Here the term took on another dimension entirely. In one of his rare journal entries in 1804, Lewis reported on September 17 how, at a site near the mouth of the White River, he had come across "immence herds of Buffaloe deer Elk and Antelopes which we saw in every direction feeding off the hills and plains. I do not think I exagerate when I estimate the number of Buffaloe which could be compreed [comprehended] at one view to amount to 3000." Throughout that summer and fall the expedition encountered numerous animals new both to them and to science, not all of whom ended up in their cooking pots. These included white-tailed jackrabbits, mule deer, coyotes, and badgers (the last creature long known to Europeans, but until Lewis and Clark encountered them along the Missouri not known to live in North America).

The abundant game did the expedition's youngest member, George Shannon, little good when he accidentally got separated from the main party at the end of August. The expedition brought four horses with it (all lost, stolen, or dead by September). Shannon had gone out to look for two stray horses. Confused, he headed north up the Missouri thinking that the party was ahead of him, when in fact it was still behind him, coming up the river. He continued heading north day after day, and the search parties sent out by the expedition could find no trace of him. Shannon, Clark wrote in his journal, was not "a first rate Hunter," and the captains feared he would starve to death on his own. He almost did. Running out of bullets, he managed to kill a rabbit by shooting a stick out of his rifle; other than that, all he had to eat for more than two weeks was wild grapes and plums he found along the river. Finally it occurred to him to try heading south, rather than continuing north, and after 16 hungry days on his own, he stumbled upon the Corps of Discovery. "Thus a man had like to have Starved to death in a land of Plenty," Clark noted in his journal on September 11.

INDIAN DIPLOMACY

In his letter of instructions to Lewis in June 1803, Thomas Jefferson had assigned many missions to the Corps of Discovery. Beyond finding the Northwest Passage, none was as important as the assignment to establish friendly relations with the Indian tribes living along the Missouri River and beyond. Before Lewis and Clark's journey was over, they would come in contact with nearly 50 different Indian tribes, some of whom had never before seen a white man, let alone an American soldier.

Men who make good soldiers are not always the same men who make good diplomats. In his letter to Lewis, Jefferson took pains to impress on the young infantry officer that he was to keep in mind his diplomatic responsibilities. He was going west to talk, not to fight. "In all your intercourse with the natives," Jefferson wrote, "treat them in the most friendly & conciliatory manner which their own conduct will admit; allay all jealousies as to the object of your journey, satisfy them of it's innocence, make them acquainted with the position, extent, character, peaceable & commercial dispositions of the U.S., of our wish to be neighborly, friendly & useful to them. . . ."

Among his other duties, Lewis was also instructed to act as a sort of tour director for prominent Native Americans. Jefferson believed that a visit to Washington, D.C., would persuade Indian leaders of the value of cooperating with the expanding American republic: "If a few of their influential chiefs, within practicable distance, wish to visit us, arrange such a visit with them. . . ."

The American West was a blank slate as far as white-Indian relations were concerned. Although neither western Indians nor white Americans had proven themselves especially peace-loving in the past, there had never been an armed conflict between the groups. If initial contacts were properly handled, Jefferson hoped, there never need be one. On the other hand, no one could predict how the western Indian tribes would react to the appearance of white strangers, however "friendly &

Daniel A. Jenks drew the Platte River and two covered wagons being ferried across it in 1859 upon arriving at a camp (also drawn) in central Wyoming. *(Library of Congress, Prints and Photographs Division [LC-USZ62-128883])*

conciliatory" their manner. If faced with superior force, Jefferson urged Lewis to return home rather than risk the loss of his own life and the life of his men in a losing battle: "In the loss of yourselves, we should lose also the information you will have acquired. . . . we wish you to err on the side of your safety . . ."

The expedition did not actually meet any Indians, friendly or otherwise, until the end of July, soon after they passed the mouth of the Platte River. Lewis and Clark knew from the information they had been given before setting out that once they reached the Platte they could expect to find villages of Otoe (Oto), Missouri, and other Indian tribes living nearby. On July 28, George Drouillard met a Missouri Indian, who told him that a mixed

village of Otoe and Missouri could be found a few days travel inland. The captains dispatched the French engagé named La Liberté, the only Otoe speaker on the expedition, to establish contact with the village.

Two days later the Corps of Discovery camped below a high bluff overlooking the Missouri, at a site near present-day Fort Calhoun, Nebraska. They raised an American flag on a pole and waited there with mounting impatience for the Otoe whom La Liberté was supposed to bringing back. What they did not know was that La Liberté had taken advantage of his orders to abandon the expedition. Eventually, Private George Gibson was dispatched to see what had become of La Liberté and the Indian delegation.

This medal is one of many distributed by the U.S. government to American Indian leaders as gestures of "peace and friendship." One side is a profile portrait of Thomas Jefferson, and the other shows clasped hands and a crossed tomahawk and peace pipe. *(American Numismatic Society, New York)*

Lewis's Air Gun ⟿

Time and again Lewis would report that the Indians they met along the way were "much astonished" by the firing of his air gun. When a weapon was fired in the early 19th century, everyone around could hear and see the results. There was a loud crack and a puff of black smoke as the gunpowder detonated. The Indians thus had good reason to be astonished when Lewis shot his specially designed weapon, and there was no noise beyond a little click and a whishing sound. Lewis's novelty weapon was built for him by a gunsmith named Isaiah Lukens in Philadelphia. Its butt was a metal chamber designed to hold compressed air, pumped in beforehand with a device Lewis carried. The air pressure could be released by pulling the trigger, and its release projected a .31-caliber bullet out the barrel of the rifle with enough force to kill small game at close range.

Finally at sunset on August 2, a French trader named Mr. Fairfong arrived at the expedition's camp, accompanied by a party of Otoe and Missouri Indians. "Capt. Lewis & myself met those Indians," Clark noted, "& informed them we were glad to See them, and would Speak to them tomorrow, Sent them Som rosted meat Pork flour & meal, in return they sent us Water millions [melons]."

The next day they met the Indian chiefs on the embankment that Lewis and Clark named Council Bluff. With Fairfong serving as translator, the captains went through a round of diplomatic gestures that would soon become routine. First they offered the Indians presents, "in perpotion [proportion] to their Consiqunce," as Clark would write. The bigger the chief, in other words, the better the present. Since Indian rank was not always as obviously established as military rank, this could create problems if the captains misjudged just who was the biggest chief, but on this occasion they seemed to have guessed right. There was one important Otoe chief missing, named Little Thief. They sent him a bundle of cloth-

ing, an American flag, and a Jefferson peace medal (a small medallion, specially produced for the expedition, which showed Thomas Jefferson's likeness on one side, and two clasped hands superimposed on the words "Peace and Friendship" on the other.) They smoked a peace pipe with the Indian chiefs, and offered each a drink of whiskey. And Lewis fired off his air gun, which much "astonished the nativs," according to Clark.

The main event, however, was Lewis's speech, his first chance to try out what became a standard oration. "Children," Lewis proclaimed, establishing his claim to superior authority in his opening line:

Commissioned and sent by the Great Chief of the Seventeen great nations of America [the United States], we have come to inform you, as we go to inform all the nations of red men who inhabit the borders of the Missouri, that a great council was lately held between this great chief of the seventeen nations of America, and your old fathers the french and the Spaniards; and that in this great council it was agreed that all the white men of Louisiana, inhabiting the waters of the Missouri and Mississippi should obey the commands of this great chief; he has accordingly adopted them as his children . . .

What was true for the white inhabitants of the Louisiana Territory also applied to the Indians, even though they had had no part in the deliberations of the "great council" that had wound up switching an old for a new father figure:

Children. From what has been said you will readily perceive, that the great chief of the Seventeen great nations of America, has become your only father; he is the only father; he is the only friend to whom you can now look for protection . . . The great chief of the Seventeen great nations of America, impelled by his parental regard for his children on the troubled waters, has sent us out to clear the road, remove every obstruction, and to make it the road of peace between himself and his red children residing there. . . .

Lewis went on in that vein at some length, with the French trader Fairfong translating, promising peace, friendship, trade, and prosperity, if the Otoe and Missouri would just heed the good advice of the representatives of the great chief of the Seventeen American nations. What Lewis's listeners made of this speech is hard to tell, but the captains perceived that they were in full agreement with its sentiments. "Those people express great Satisfa[ct]ion at the Speech Delivered," Clark wrote in his journal that evening, his own sense of satisfaction with the day's proceedings very evident.

On August 19, further up the Missouri, they met another party of Otoe and Missouri, this time including Little Thief, who had been missing on August 3, and a Missouri chief named Big Horse. Once again Lewis gave his speech and showed off the airgun. The present-giving did not work out quite as well this time, however: Big Horse felt he had been given less recognition by the whites than had Little Thief. The captains explained patiently that the real rewards were yet to come, when a peaceable trade network of all the Indian tribes was established stretching up the Missouri. The Otoe and Missouri were more concerned with the here and now than the golden future that the captains promised. They wanted to know how much of the rich treasure trove found in the expedition's three boats would be passed on to them before the white men left and distributed the remaining goods to other Indian tribes who they regarded as rivals if not enemies. Clark's description of the outcome of this council was less glowing than the one he had written two weeks before. The Indians, obviously displeased, hung around the camp long after the captains had politely suggested they go away and "beged much for wishey [whiskey]."

On August 30, at Calumet bluff, near the present-day site of Gavins Point Dam in Nebraska, they held their third council, this time with chiefs of the Yankton Nakota Sioux tribe. The Sioux (Dakota, Lakota, Nakota) Indians' formidable reputation on the plains had spread all the way to Washington, D.C. President Jefferson had stressed the importance of making "a friendly impression" on the Sioux, "because of their immense power." The Sioux were composed of the Dakota, Lakota, and Nakota, each of which was made up of bands. Collectively and historically they were known as the Sioux but this was not the name the group used for themselves. The Sioux— especially the Lakota who lived farther west than the Dakota—were renowned as buffalo hunters and as mounted warriors. Many of the images that define popular memory in the United States of the Indians and their way of life, including the tipi and feathered headdresses, comes from the practices of the Lakota, as well as other nomadic tribes who lived further to the west like the Comanche and the Cheyenne.

The Sioux were divided into numerous groups or bands speaking separate dialects. The Yankton Nakota occupied a region between the Missouri River and Minnesota. Though buffalo hunters, they also maintained some semipermanent villages. They were well disposed to white traders coming up the Mis-

souri and gave Lewis and Clark a friendly reception. Pierre Dorion, a French trader who had been traveling upriver with the expedition since June, and who had lived among the Yankton for many years, acted as translator.

The talk about one Great White Father taking the place of another was probably just as confusing to the Yankton as it had been to the other tribes who had already heard Lewis's speech. And, as had been the case at the last council with the Missouri and the Otoe, the

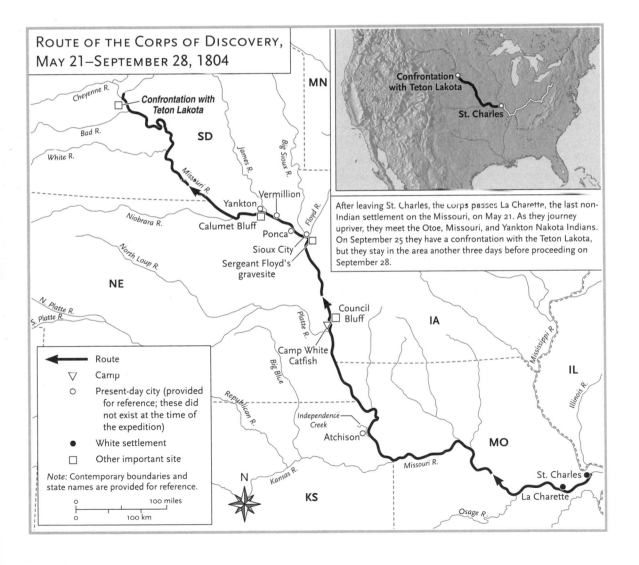

ROUTE OF THE CORPS OF DISCOVERY, MAY 21–SEPTEMBER 28, 1804

After leaving St. Charles, the corps passes La Charette, the last non-Indian settlement on the Missouri, on May 21. As they journey upriver, they meet the Otoe, Missouri, and Yankton Nakota Indians. On September 25 they have a confrontation with the Teton Lakota, but they stay in the area another three days before proceeding on September 28.

Route
Camp
Present-day city (provided for reference; these did not exist at the time of the expedition)
White settlement
Other important site

Note: Contemporary boundaries and state names are provided for reference.

100 miles
100 km

Yankton could not understand why the whites were so stingy in distributing the riches they carried in their boats. The captains' explanation that they came not as traders themselves but as explorers with a long way yet to travel did not make much sense to their listeners. But the chiefs responded favorably to the promise of the trade that would soon come their way from St. Louis, and one of their chiefs agreed to travel east to Washington, D.C., with Pierre Dorion the following year to meet this Great White Father that Lewis had spoken of so glowingly. Before the council ended, one of the Yankton passed along a friendly warning to Lewis and Clark about their cousins upstream, the Teton Lakota. According to Half Moon, a Yankton chief: "I fear those nations above will not open their ears, and you cannot, I fear[,] open them." The captains quietly decided not to send Corporal Warfington and his detachment of soldiers back down the Missouri to St. Louis that fall as they had earlier planned. They might need every rifle they could muster in the weeks ahead.

When they embarked on their diplomatic mission, Lewis and Clark set off with an oversimplified understanding of how Indian economies functioned along the Missouri. The Indians, they reasoned, had something the whites wanted, which was furs; the whites had something the Indians wanted, which was manufactured goods. Therefore, they believed, increased trade between whites and Indians seemed to be in everyone's interests, and that fact alone, once properly understood, should have been enough to ensure peaceful relations between whites and Indians.

But things proved more complicated. A U.S. diplomat on the Missouri could no more assume that the economic interests of the various Indian tribes were identical than a U.S. diplomat in Europe could assume that those of the English, French, Dutch, and Spanish coincided. The Teton Lakota lived on both sides of the Missouri and ranged far to the west across the Plains in hunting and raiding parties. At the same time, they played a key role in the trade system of the upper Missouri River. They were intermediaries in that system, acquiring manufactured goods from other Dakota, Lakota, and Nakota groups who had direct contact with British traders in Canada and trading those goods to the tribes of Indians who lived a more settled existence as farmers along the upper Missouri River. Unlike the Yankton Nakota, the prospect of white traders coming up the Missouri thus seemed to the Teton an economic threat, not a welcome source of additional goods. Their own role in the upper Missouri River trading system would be undercut by an inflow of American manufactured goods passing directly into the hands of tribes living along the Missouri such as the Arikara, Mandan, and Hidatsa.

The Corps of Discovery had their long-anticipated and half-dreaded encounter with the Teton Lakota on September 24 at the mouth of the Bad River (near present-day Fort Pierre, South Dakota). The captains invited the Teton chiefs to come to a council on the riverside the next day. They hoped for the best, but as Clark noted in his journal that evening, they had "prepared all things for Action in Case of necessity." The fact that the expedition's last remaining horse was stolen by some Teton warriors that day did not bode well for what was to come.

The next morning, the expedition nervously awaited their guests on a sandbar at the mouth of the Bad River. The men had set up an awning to shade the captains and the chiefs during the council, and they raised the American flag on a pole stuck in the sand. By late morning three Teton chiefs, Black Buffalo, the Partisan, and Buffalo Medicine, had arrived. There were also several hundred Teton who came and looked down at the white men from the riverbanks. Pierre Cruzatte, whose command of the Teton dialect was distinctly lim-ited, acted as translator. Lewis gave his speech, and then the captains ordered their men to parade by, in their dress uniforms, with their rifles on their shoulders.

Then it came time to hand out gifts to the chiefs. Having decided that Black Buffalo was the Teton's most important leader, the cap-tains presented him with a lavish offering of gifts. The other two chiefs, especially the one known as the Partisan, felt slighted by com-parison. The Partisan and Buffalo Medicine became surly. Black Buffalo, feeling that he could not allow the other chiefs to outdo him in willingness to stand up to the whites, added his own voice to their demands that the expe-dition hand over more of its goods, perhaps even one of the pirogues. The captains were not prepared to be quite that generous but, perhaps remembering Jefferson's insistence that they convey to the Indians how "neigh-borly, friendly & useful" the United States could be, invited the three chiefs and some of their men on board the keelboat, which was anchored offshore. They also offered the chiefs a small glass of whisky each. That proved to be a mistake.

Pretending he was drunk, the Partisan became "troublesome," in what Clark later described "as a Cloak for his rascally inten-tions." With some difficulty, the captains man-aged to get the chiefs off the keelboat and on board one of the pirogues, and he ferried them back to shore. Clark went along, while Lewis remained in command on the keelboat. As the pirogue touched land, three Teton war-riors grabbed hold of its bow cable, while the Partisan pushed up against Clark and declared that the whites could not proceed any further up river because "he had not receved presents sufficent from us." With that, Clark's capacity for the diplomatic niceties hit its limit. He drew his sword. Sergeant John Ordway recorded what happened next:

Capt Clark spoke to all the party to Stand to their arms. Capt Lewis who was on board [the keelboat] ordered every man to his arms. The large Swivel loaded immediately with 16 Musquet balls in it, the two other Swivels loaded well with Buck Shot [and] each of them manned.

The Indians watching from the riverbanks strung their bows and took aim at the corps. At that moment Black Buffalo stepped in. Unlike the Partisan, he did not seem eager for a fight. He ordered his warriors to release the pirogue's cable, which he took in his own hands. Clark, uncertain of Black Buffalo's intentions, spoke sternly, warning him, as Ordway recounted, "that we must and would go on . . . that we were not Squaws, but war-riors." Black Buffalo replied that "he had war-riors too and if we were to go on they would follow us and kill and take the whole of us by degrees."

The corps had the better weapons, but they were badly outnumbered. At any moment, anger, pride, or an itchy trigger fin-ger could have unleashed a hail of gunfire and arrows that would have left many men dead on both sides. It was Black Buffalo who found the way to defuse the confrontation. He sud-denly asked Clark if the women and children of his tribe would be able to visit the keelboat. Clark agreed, and, honor satisfied by this con-cession, Black Buffalo let go of the cable. The two sides lowered their weapons and the cri-sis passed. Black Buffalo and two warriors came along on the keelboat to spend the night with the expedition. The Corps moved upriver to an island landing where most of them slept poorly. "I call this Island bad humered island," Clark later wrote, "as we were in a bad humor."

The next day, at Black Buffalo's invitation, they visited his village. Lewis went on shore with some of the party, while Clark remained on board the keelboat, anchored well offshore for safety. Eventually deciding that Black Buffalo's intentions were friendly, for the moment at least, Clark joined Lewis in the village. All that day and long into the night there was feasting and speeches and dancing, and a pre-

tense on both sides that the unpleasantness of the day before had never happened. But it was several days later before the expedition stopped watching the shore nervously for a Teton ambush. The Teton Lakota, Clark declared, were "the pirates of the Missouri,"

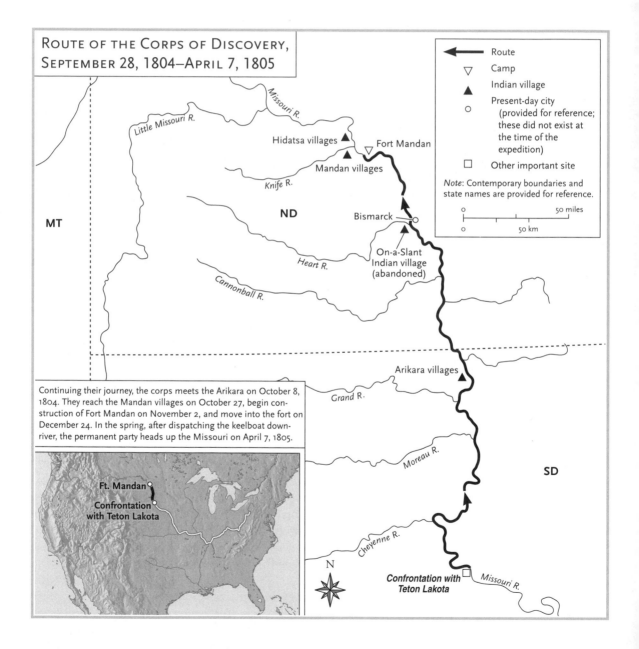

ROUTE OF THE CORPS OF DISCOVERY, SEPTEMBER 28, 1804–APRIL 7, 1805

←	Route
▽	Camp
▲	Indian village
○	Present-day city (provided for reference; these did not exist at the time of the expedition)
☐	Other important site

Note: Contemporary boundaries and state names are provided for reference.

0   50 miles
0   50 km

Missouri R.
Little Missouri R.
Hidatsa villages ▲
Mandan villages ▲
▽ Fort Mandan
Knife R.
MT
ND
Bismarck ○
On-a-Slant Indian village (abandoned)
Heart R.
Cannonball R.

Continuing their journey, the corps meets the Arikara on October 8, 1804. They reach the Mandan villages on October 27, begin construction of Fort Mandan on November 2, and move into the fort on December 24. In the spring, after dispatching the keelboat downriver, the permanent party heads up the Missouri on April 7, 1805.

Arikara villages ▲
Grand R.

Ft. Mandan ○
Confrontation with Teton Lakota ○

Moreau R.
SD

Cheyenne R.
N
Confrontation with Teton Lakota ☐
Missouri R.

and he foresaw nothing but trouble with them in the future until the United States made them "feel a dependence on its will for their supply of merchandise."

On October 8, near the mouth of the Grand River, the Corps of Discovery encountered a tribe more to their liking. The Arikara were farmers growing corn and tobacco. They lived in earthen lodges in permanent settlements. For white explorers who were a long way from home, coming across such a village offered a reassuring glimpse of stability and a pattern of life familiar to those who had grown up in rural Virginia and Kentucky. "All Tranquillity," Clark recorded in his journal after three days in the company of the Arikara. Good relations were furthered by presence of a good interpreter, Joseph Gravelines, a French fur trader who had been living with the Arikara. Lewis gave his speech, gifts were distributed, peace pipes smoked. Some of the men in the expedition enjoyed even closer relations with the Arikara women, who, as Clark observed in his journal without further comment, were "very fond of carressing our men."

York's presence on the expedition had gone virtually unmentioned in the journals until the Arikara noticed him and decided that he was by far the most fascinating member of the Corps of Discovery. "Those Indians wer much astonished at my Servent," Clark noted on October 10, "they never Saw a black man before, all flocked around him & examind him from top to toe, he Carried on the joke and made himself more turribal than we wished him to doe." York enjoyed the attention, especially from the younger Arikara, and pretended to be a bear in human form. "The children would follow after him," John Ordway wrote, "& if he turned towards them, they would run from him & hollow [holler] as if they were terrefied, & afraid of him."

TO THE MANDAN VILLAGES

On October 12, the Corps of Discovery bade farewell to the Arikara and set off once again up the Missouri. The weather was turning cold. Clark, suffering from rheumatism, felt its effects cruelly. Their late start that spring and the frequent halts to hold councils with Indian tribes had put the expedition behind schedule. The captains decided that they would not be able to travel farther than the known and mapped portion of the Missouri before making their winter encampment.

On October 24, it snowed a little in the morning. Clark's rheumatism felt a bit improved, he reported in the journal. Later that day, at a location along the Missouri north of present-day Bismarck, North Dakota, Lewis and Clark met a Mandan chief named Sheheke, or Big White, who was out hunting along the river. They met "with great Cordiallity & Sermony [ceremony]." They smoked a peace pipe on shore and later invited Sheheke and his brother aboard the keelboat "for a few minits."

The next day, October 25, other Mandan rode downriver on horseback to marvel at the sight of the non-Indian newcomers. "Indeed," Clark wrote in his journal, "they are continuelly in Sight Satisfying their Curriossities as to our apperance &c." The trees along the river were now bare of leaves.

On October 26 they arrived at Sheheke's village, known as Mitunka, and made their camp. The Mandan were delighted at the arrival of the expedition. Never before had such a large party of non-Indians come up the river to the Mandan villages. "Many men women Children flocked down to See us," Clark wrote in his journal. Clark's rheumatism was acting up again, and he stayed at the keelboat while Lewis walked to the village with Sheheke. But other Mandan chiefs came to smoke peace pipes with Clark and marveled at the men's possessions, including a steel

On their return journey, Lewis and Clark convinced Big White to go to Washington to meet Thomas Jefferson and discuss trade possibilities with the United States. Clark gave Big White non-Indian clothing for this journey. Wi-Jun-Jon, an Assiniboine chief shown here, also wore white men's clothing when he visited Washington in about 1837. *(Library of Congress, Prints and Photographs Division [LC-USZC2-3313])*

mill they had brought along to grind corn. Clark noted the Mandan were also "delighted" at the sight of "my black Servent," York. All in all, things were going well. The Corps of Discovery had traveled 1,600 miles up the Missouri since setting off under that "jentle brease" nearly five and a half months earlier. They could go no further in 1804. The Mandan would be their neighbors until spring returned.

5

"THE MOST PERFECT HARMONEY"
Winter at Fort Mandan

As Captains Lewis and Clark contemplated the tasks that lay before them in settling their men into winter quarters on the farthest western frontier ever explored by Americans, the man who had sent them there, President Jefferson, was attending to his official duties in the capital of the United States. They were more than 1,000 miles and, seemingly, worlds apart. But it is worth noting that Lewis and Clark would have more neighbors in their immediate vicinity that winter than would Jefferson. Four thousand people lived in Washington, D.C., in 1804; some 4,500 lived in the five villages occupied by members of the Mandan and Hidatsa tribes. These villages were the center of a vast trading network stretching across much of the northern half of the Louisiana Territory, and as such they had long served as a magnet for French and British traders venturing south from Canada. Together, the villages constituted a frontier metropolis, a center of trade and diplomatic intrigue, and the most important permanent community of Native Americans that the Corps of Discovery would encounter on their journey across the continent.

THE MANDAN VILLAGES

Since the early 18th century, the Mandan villages had been one of the few geographical reference points along the upper Missouri River known to Europeans and white Americans. A French explorer named Pierre La Verendrye undertook several notable efforts in the 1730s to find a route across the North American continent to the Pacific. He failed to find an overland route on a 1731 expedition, but he was interested afterward to hear from Indians of a river flowing from the west that might serve as a water route (he did not realize this was the same river whose mouth on the Mississippi had been discovered by his countrymen Marquette and Joliet a half-century earlier). In 1738 La Verendrye headed south from a fur trading post in the valley of the Assiniboine River in New France to see if he could find it. La Verendrye had also been intrigued by rumors of a tribe of fair-skinned, "civilized" Indians living along river he sought. He found the Missouri, and with it nine populous villages of Mandan Indians, then located near the mouth of the Heart River. La Verendrye failed to discover the Northwest Passage, but the journal of his trip provided

By painting Hidatsa Indians as various as young male hunters, mothers carrying their children, an old man with a rifle, and a bundled figure resting beneath a tree, Karl Bodmer was able to depict the condensed and eclectic population of the Hidatsa village in this 1833 painting entitled *Winter Village of the Manitaries (Hidatsa) in Dakota Territory. (National Archives [NWDNS-111-SC-92845])*

With their village looming on a cliff behind them, a few Hidatsa Indians are shown here in dugout canoes, probably fishing to bring food back to the tribe. *(Library of Congress, Prints and Photographs Division [LC-USZ62-28804])*

Europeans with their first glimpse of the Mandan and their potential importance as trading partners along the Missouri.

As a group, the Mandan tribe was, in fact, paler-skinned and lighter-haired than many other Indians, and Mandan also seemed more "European" to the explorers who encountered them than did other Plains Indians because of their preference for a sedentary, agriculture, and trade-based economy. In time, this gave rise to a myth that the Mandan were the likely descendants of a legendary Welsh king who had supposedly brought hundreds of his subjects to the New World centuries before Columbus's arrival. Among his many other instructions to Lewis, Thomas Jefferson had urged him to determine whether there was any truth to this tale of the Mandan's supposed Welsh ancestry.

Mandan fortunes took a turn for the worse toward the end of the 18th century, when the tribe's numbers were greatly reduced by smallpox epidemics. With a smaller population, the villagers could no longer easily fend off raids by hostile nomadic tribes. For safety's sake, the survivors abandoned their old villages near the mouth of the Heart River where La Verendrye had found them and moved about 60 miles further up the Missouri to their present location near the mouth of the Knife

The Mandan Indians lived in earthen lodges like the one shown above in a photograph taken by Edward Curtis in the early 20th century. *(Library of Congress, Prints and Photographs Division [LC-USZ62-114582])*

River. The Mandan now lived in just two villages. The southernmost of these, located on the west bank of the Missouri, was called Mitutanka. Its chief was Sheheke, or Big White (so called because he was both pale and fat); he was the Mandan chief whom Lewis and Clark had met along with his hunting party on the Missouri. Further up the river, on the east bank, was the second Mandan village, Nuptadi. Its chief was Black Cat. A little farther west, along the banks of the Knife River, lay three Hidatsa villages, whose important chiefs included Black Moccasin and Le Borgne, also known as One Eye. (The Hidatsa were known by various other names, depending on which village they belonged to; Lewis and Clark called some of them Minnetaree, and others Wattason or Ahaharway. To simplify things, they will all be referred to here as Hidatsa, the name that remains in current usage.)

To outward appearance there was not much to distinguish the villages occupied by the two main tribes: Each consisted of a collection of dome-shaped earthen lodges clustered together for protection within low wooden palisades and surrounded by fields in which they grew corn and other crops. But the tribes spoke distinct languages, and differed in other ways that would prove to have great significance to the future success of Lewis and Clark's expedition. While the Mandan rarely ventured far from their home villages, Hidatsa warriors ventured out on raiding parties hundreds of miles to the west—as far as the headwaters of the Missouri on the eastern slopes of a distant mountain range.

PROMISES OF PEACE AND TRADE

As always when they encountered new Indian tribes, the first thing Lewis and Clark did was set up a formal council meeting. They hired a locally based French-Canadian trader, René Jessaume, as interpreter; he had lived among the Mandan and Arikara for many years, and he had a Mandan wife. (Jessaume and his wife would move into the expedition's quarters that winter so that his services as an interpreter would always be available.) The captains scheduled the council meeting for October 28. But high winds and blowing sands forced a postponement to the next day, and it also kept some of the most important Mandan and Hidatsa chiefs from attending. So the meeting was rescheduled.

On October 29, at a site on the eastern bank of the Missouri across from the Mandan village of Mitutanka, Mandan and Hidatsa assembled to hear what the white strangers had to say. The captains made the usual speeches and presented the usual medals. Lewis fired the air gun, which drew the usual astonished response. But, as had also happened before, Lewis and Clark had a hard time persuading their audience that an era of peaceful relations among the Missouri River tribes, guaranteed by the new Great White Father in the East, was really at hand. An

Arikara Indian had come up the Missouri with Lewis and Clark as a peace delegate, and, encouraged by the captains, pledged his tribe's peaceful intentions for the future. The Mandan, who generally avoided warfare unless attacked, would have liked to believe their southern flank was now secure from attack. But they remained skeptical about the value of promises offered by "liars and bad men" like the Arikara.

If Lewis and Clark's promises of peace seemed overblown to their Indian listeners, their promises of trade goods coming up the Missouri from St. Louis sparked genuine enthusiasm, particularly among the Mandan. More traders bringing more goods in competition with the British traders from the Hudson's Bay company and the North West Company would work to the economic advantage of the Mandan. Black Cat and Big White, the principal Mandan chiefs, made it clear to Lewis and Clark that they were welcome to spend the winter. What it took the captains a while to realize was the Mandan were also angling to

---

Smallpox and the Fate of the Mandan Tribe ⌒

Before the coming of the white men, North American Indian tribes suffered little from epidemic diseases. Smallpox, a contagious disease with a high mortality rate, arrived with British settlers on the eastern seaboard in the 17th century. Smallpox, to which the Indians had no developed immunity as some Europeans had, devastated many eastern tribes and followed white settlement inland. In 1781 the Mandan had been hard hit by a smallpox epidemic spread by increasing contact with whites. But worse was to come in 1837, when a steamboat traveling up the Missouri carried a new round of infection. This time the Mandan population was reduced to a mere 150 survivors. Other tribes suffered similar losses. After the epidemic ran its course, remnants of the Hidatsa and Mandan banded together in one village; later joined by the Arikara, they became known as the Three Affiliated Tribes. Their descendants live today on the Fort Berthold Reservation in North Dakota.

cut their closest Indian neighbors out of the deal; the Mandan spread rumors among the Hidatsa that the whites were up to no good, perhaps even planning an attack on their villages in alliance with the Sioux. While Black Cat and Big White frequently visited the captains that winter, the Hidatsa chiefs stayed away.

WINTER QUARTERS

Their council concluded, Lewis and Clark turned their attention to the ever more pressing task of getting their men under cover. By November 3 the enlisted men were constructing the fort that would be their winter home on the eastern bank of the Missouri across from Mitutanka and seven miles below the mouth of the Knife River. Fort Mandan was a triangular structure. Sergeant Gass, the expedition's master carpenter, left a detailed description of its design and construction in his journal:

> The following is the manner in which our fort and huts were built; the huts were in two rows, containing four rooms each, and joined at one end forming an angle. When rasied [raised] about 7 feet high a floor of [split planks] were laid, and covered with grass and clay; which made a warm loft. The upper part [of the huts] projected a foot over and the roofs were made shed-fashion, rising from the inner side, and making the outer wall about 18 feet high . . . In the angle formed by the two rows of huts we built two rooms, for holding our provisions and stores.

The expedition's master carpenter, Sergeant Patrick Gass, included a detailed description and etching of the process of building a line of huts, perhaps Fort Mandan and adjoining shelter, in his journal. *(Library of Congress, Prints and Photographs Division [LC-USZ62-19230])*

This view into the interior of the hut of a Mandan chief shows a group of Indians sitting on buffalo robes watching the central figure who is illuminated by the sunlight that sifts through a hole at the top of the lodge. To the left the artist included the horses, which were kept inside to protect them from inclement weather and thieves. *(Library of Congress, Prints and Photographs Division [LC-USZ62-2086])*

The third side of the triangle consisted of a high log fence with a gate in the middle. The fort would be home that winter to 35 soldiers: Lewis and Clark and 26 enlisted men who would go west with them, plus Corporal Warfington and six soldiers who would accompany him in the keelboat back to St. Louis in the spring. There were also a number of civilians who would live in the fort, including York and Drouillard, Jessaume and his Mandan wife, and others yet to arrive. The French engagés had been discharged and paid off by the time Fort Mandan was under construction; a few stayed at the fort, while others spent the winter with the Mandan and Hidatsa or headed down the Missouri to stay at the Arikara villages with a French trader, Joseph Gravelines. Another addition to the fort's inhabitants was a French trapper they met at the Mandan villages, Jean-Baptiste Lepage, who on a previous trapping expedition had traveled a few dozen miles farther up the Missouri; the captains persuaded him to enlist in the U.S. Army, and he became part of the permanent party that would set out westward the following spring.

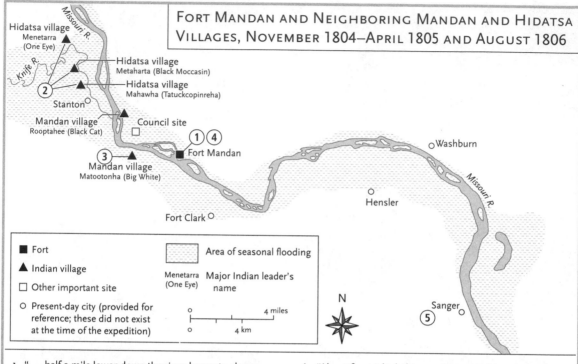

FORT MANDAN AND NEIGHBORING MANDAN AND HIDATSA VILLAGES, NOVEMBER 1804–APRIL 1805 AND AUGUST 1806

1. "... half a mile lower down the river, began to clear a place for a camp and fort. We pitched our tents and laid the foundation of one line of huts."
   —Patrick Gass, November 2, 1804

2. "The Indians in all the towns and camps treated Captain Lewis and the party with great respect, except one of the principal chiefs ... Horned Weasel, Who did not chuse to be seen by the Capt., and left word that he was not at home, &c."
   — William Clark, November 27, 1804

3. "... went up to the 1st village of Mandans to dance ... carried with us a fiddle & a Tambereen & a Sounden horn, ... So we danced in different lodges until late in the afternoon. then a part of the men returned to the fort. the remainder Stayed all night in the village."
   —John Ordway, January 1, 1805

4. "About five o'clock this evening, one of the wives of Charbonneau was delivered of a fine boy. . . . her labor was tedious and the pain violent. . . . he administered two rings of [rattlesnake] to the woman, broken in small pieces with the fingers, and added to a small quantity of water. . . . she had not taken it more than ten minutes, before she brought forth."
   —Meriwether Lewis, February 11, 1805

5. "We do not go on so rapidly as we did higher up the river: but having lashed our small canoes together, we go on very safe and can make fifty or sixty miles a day. Captain Lewis is getting much better and we are all in good spirits. . . . and we proceeded on, . . ."
   —Patrick Gass, August 19, 1806

Note: Original spelling and punctuation have been retained from journal entries.

The men building the fort needed little encouragement to work hard. By the last week of November, they were sleeping under the roofs of their newly competed huts—just in time, as it turned out, because snow was by now beginning to fall regularly. Clark recorded 13 inches on the ground November 29. By the first week of December the Missouri River was covered with ice. The keelboat and pirogues were frozen at the water's edge (the captains' failure to have the boats dragged ashore before the freeze seems a serious misjudgment). If there had been any doubt in the minds of the Corps of Discovery as to how completely they were cut off from the world they had left behind the previous May, the sight of the newly frozen river must surely have dispelled it. No matter what happened, there was no retreat now until spring came.

The days were short, and the brief appearance of the winter sun provided little warmth. On December 7 Clark recorded in his journal that the temperature was 44 degrees "below Breizing [freezing]" in the morning (or 12 degrees below zero). Before the winter was over it would get a lot colder, down to 42 degrees below zero. With few trees to block the wind blowing down from the Canadian prairies, the windchill effect could have deadly consequences. "Our rooms are verry close and warm," Sergeant Ordway wrote of the huts in the fort, "So we can keep ourselves warm and comfortable, but the Sentinel who stood out in the open weather had to be relieved every hour. . . ." Any trip outside could have painful consequences. Toes, fingers, and ears froze. The captains soon became expert at treating frostbite, and none of the men seem to have lost any vital body parts.

When the men were not on duty, they relaxed with the simple pleasures available to them. They played backgammon or socialized with the Indians (chiefly Mandan) who came in large numbers almost every day to witness the curious novelty of a large number of white men living together in their midst. Many times the Indian visitors would spend the night. When darkness fell Cruzatte would bring out his fiddle to entertain the expedition members and their guests; as Clark noted in his journal toward the end of the winter, "fiew nights pass without a Dance." The heavens

also provided some entertainment; the men were treated to a display of the northern lights in November, and a total eclipse of the Moon in January.

An army, it is often said, travels on its stomach. In this case the army was sitting still, but the men still needed to eat prodigiously to keep up their energy in the bitter cold. Fortunately, supplying food was never much of a problem at Fort Mandan, especially not in the early months of winter. Hunting parties brought in buffalo, deer, and antelope, some killed within sight of the fort. The Corps of Discovery also traded with the local Indians for corn. The expedition blacksmiths, John Shields and Alexander Willard, set up a forge with bellows and anvil just after Christmas, and they started to both repair and manufacture iron goods for trade. The Mandan particularly desired iron war axes, for which they eagerly traded their dried corn.

Unlike the previous winter at Camp Wood, discipline was not a problem at Fort Mandan. The captains had established their authority over the men and won their loyalty. There was only one court-martial, of a man who climbed over the wall of the fort rather than ask to be admitted at the gate. Though he was sentenced to 50 lashes, the sentence was never carried out. That would prove the last court-martial Lewis and Clark convened. At winter's end Lewis would be able to write proudly to Jefferson:

> every individual of the party are in good health, and excellent sperits; zealously attatched to the enterprise, and anxious to proceed; not a whisper of discontent or murmur is to be heard among them; but all in unison, act with the most perfect harmoney. With such men I have every thing to hope, and but little to fear.

While the enlisted men carried out the routine tasks of garrison duty, the captains had their own business to attend to. First of all, they had to tie up some of the diplomatic loose ends left over from their council meeting in October. Lewis and Clark realized that the Hidatsa had felt slighted by them since their arrival, and they worried that because so many British traders lived in their midst, the Hidatsa would favor the Hudson's Bay and North West Companies over potential U.S. rivals. In late November Lewis went up to the Hidatsa villages to win them over. He handed out gifts and assured the Hidatsa chiefs that, notwithstanding the rumors passed along by the Mandan, the expedition's intentions were strictly peaceful. Trade with the Americans, he assured the Hidatsa, would work to the benefit of both the Mandan and their tribe. He also won a promise from some of the Hidatsa chiefs to make peace with their western enemies, the Shoshone and Blackfeet (a promise they were happy to offer to the gift-bearing white men since it cost them nothing and in any case had little intention of keeping it).

At the Mandan villages Lewis and Clark faced a new diplomatic challenge: establish-

The Trading Network of the Plains Indians

The tribes who lived in more or less permanent agricultural villages along the Missouri River, including the Mandan, Hidatsa, Arikara, Pawnee, Wichita, and Omaha, were linked to the nomadic, buffalo-hunting groups such as the Lakota and Nakota in a vast and intricate trade network. The nomadic tribes would bring buffalo hides to annual gatherings at the agricultural villages to trade for food and tobacco, and for manufactured goods that came down from Canada and up from St. Louis. Just how far-reaching this trade extended became clear to the captains when they were returning from the Pacific in 1806 and found one of the battle axes that John Shields had manufactured at Fort Mandan in the winter of 1805 in the hands of the Nez Perce Indians, on the western side of the Rockies.

In the "Estimate of the Eastern Indians," which the captains sent back to Washington in spring 1805, they offered a detailed description of how the Mandan Indians fit in to the Plains trading network. The Mandan, they wrote,

> live in fortified villages . . . and cultivate corn, beans, squashes and tobacco, which form articles of traffic with their natives the Assiniboin [a Canadian tribe]: they also barter horses with the Assiniboins for arms, ammunition, axes, kettles, and other articles of European manufacture, which these last obtain from the British establishments on the Assiniboin river.

The Mandan then bartered the European goods for horses and "leather tents" (by which they probably meant buffalo skins), from western Indian tribes, including the Crow and Cheyenne "who visit them occasionally for the purpose of traffic."

ing and maintaining proper relations with the British traders from the Hudson's Bay and North West Companies who came down from Canada to do business with the Mandan and Hidatsa. This was one area in which Jefferson had not provided any guidance in his 1803 letter of instruction to Lewis, beyond expressing the hope that any British traders they "may happen to meet" would be prepared to extend them "friendly aid." He had not anticipated that the Corps of Discovery would settle down for its winter encampment in a major trading center such as the Mandan villages where they would have the opportunity for extended conversations and interaction with the British.

Lewis had a hard time disguising his deep and long-held anti-British sentiments; he had not forgiven them for his father's death in the Revolution. But, along with Clark, he did his best to assure the British traders that, notwithstanding the transfer of the Louisiana Territory to U.S. control, they were still welcome to do business with the Indian tribes along the Missouri River. However, they did insist that the British should no longer hand out medals or the British flag as gifts to the Indians, because that would only confuse the tribes as

European (and, increasingly, American) goods such as muskets, iron pots, metal fishhooks, and woven cloth made life easier for the Indians in this trade network. But they also encouraged a new and more wasteful attitude toward natural resources as Indians began to overhunt their territories for the animal hides and furs valued by the Europeans.

Buffalo hides were versatile assets in the trade network; they could be used as tipi covers, clothing, robes, and bedding. They were also used to transport family belongings during travel. *(Bureau of Land Management)*

to which Great White Father they owed their ultimate allegiance. If Lewis and Clark had anything to say on the matter, there would be no more Indian chiefs in the Louisiana Territory bedecked in medals bearing the likeness of King George.

The British traders (a number of whom were Frenchmen in the service of the British fur trading companies), offered no challenge to U.S. authority and indeed provided the captains with some valuable services. Hugh McCracken of the North West Company agreed to carry a letter from Lewis to the Assiniboine Indians and the traders who lived among them at the North West Company outpost 150 miles away in Canada, advising them of the Louisiana Purchase and its implications for the future of trade in the region. McCracken and other British traders also provided Lewis and Clark with a great deal of useful geographical information. Clark noted in his journal in mid-December that a trader named Hugh Heney had given them "Some Scetches of the Countrey between the Mississippi & Missouri," and even more important, "Some Sketches . . . which he had obtained from the Indins, to the *West* of this place." So Anglo-American diplomatic relations in this remote corner of the Louisiana Territory could be described as proper that winter, even if they never were entirely friendly. "Captain Lewis could not make himself agreeable to us," North West Company trader Charles MacKenzie complained after visiting Fort Mandan in January 1805. "He could speak fluently and learnedly on all subjects, but his inveterate disposition against the British stained, at least in our eyes, all his eloquence."

TAKING STOCK

The captains now had the opportunity to set down a detailed account of all that they had learned on their journey thus far up the Missouri River. In spring Corporal Warfington and his detachment would take the keelboat back to St. Louis, the last chance Lewis and Clark would have to communicate the wonders they had thus far seen to President Jefferson, until their own return from the Pacific.

Clark went back over his journal entries and the reports he had gotten since from Indians and British traders and drew up the most accurate map yet available of the wandering trail of the Missouri River between St. Louis and the Mandan villages. Lewis wrote out a "summary view of the rivers and creeks which discharge themselves into the Missouri . . ." which, in addition to describing the location of the river junctions they had passed, contained a great deal of carefully observed if somewhat miscellaneous observations about the character of the various rivers ("The river Platte does not furnish the Missouri with it's colouring matter, as has been asserted by some," Lewis wrote, "but it throws into it immence quantities of sand, and gives a celerity to it's current, of which it does not abate untill it joins the Mississippi").

Lewis and Clark reported on and prepared to send back samples of 108 types of plants and seeds they had gathered en route. They reported on and prepared to send back samples of 68 types of minerals they had dug out along the shoreline of the Missouri. They labeled and prepared to send back samples of the animals they had encountered thus far, including bones, horns, animal hides, and a few live specimens of smaller and more transportable creatures, including the prairie dog, which must have spent a boring winter in his little cage. They boxed up Clark's journal and prepared to send it back as a record of their own efforts since first proceeding on up the Missouri.

to the Senate & House of Representatives of the United States.

In pursuance of a measure proposed to Congress by a message of Jan. 18. 1803. and sanctioned by their appropriation for carrying it into execution, Capt. Meriwether Lewis of the 1st regiment of infantry was appointed, with a party of men, to explore the river Missouri, from it's mouth to it's source, & crossing the highlands by the shortest portage, to seek the best water communication thence to the Pacific ocean: & Lieut. Clarke was appointed second in command. they were to enter into conference with the Indian nations on their route, with a view to the establishment of commerce with them. they entered the Missouri May 14. 1804. and on the 1st of Nov. took up their winter quarters near the Mandan towns, 1609 miles above the mouth of the river, in Lat. 47°-21'-47" North, & Long. 99°-24'-45" West from Greenwich. on the 8th of April 1805. they proceeded up the river in pursuance of the objects prescribed to them. a letter of the preceding day Apr. 7. from Capt. Lewis, is herewith communicated. during his stay among the Mandans, he had been able to lay down the Missouri according to courses & distances taken on his passage up it, corrected by frequent observations of Longitude & Latitude; & to add to the actual survey of this portion of the river, a general map of the country between the Missisipi & Pacific, from the 34th to the 54th degrees of Latitude. these additions are from information collected from Indians with whom he had opportunities of communicating, during his journey & residence with them.

On February 19, 1806, Thomas Jefferson drafted a letter to the U.S. Congress informing the members of the discoveries of Lewis and Clark. *(National Archives [NWL-46-PRESMESS9AE2-2])*

Perhaps their greatest contribution to the knowledge of Americans about the new Louisiana Territory was a report they prepared and entitled "Estimate of Eastern Indians," summarizing all that they had learned, through direct observation or from reports by others, of dozens of Indian tribes and bands living along the Missouri. They reported on the location of the various tribes, their economies, their customs, their attitudes toward whites, and their relations with other Indians. There was much valuable anthropological and historical information in this "estimate," but as official representatives of the United States, Lewis and Clark obviously intended their report first and foremost to serve the trade and diplomatic purposes of their government, rather than the cause of science. The captains had their clear favorites and villains among the Indians they described. Thus they drew a stark contrast between the character of two groups they had met on the Missouri, the Arikara and the Teton Lakota: "Though they [the Arikara] be the oldest inhabitants [living along their territory on the shore of the Missouri] they may properly be considered the farmers or *tenants at will* of that lawless, savage and rapacious race the Sioux *Teton*, who rob them of their horses, plunder their gardens and fields, and sometimes murder them. . . . If these people were freed from the oppression of the Tetons, their trade would increase rapidly. . . ."

Jefferson thought so highly of the "estimate" when he received it late in 1805 that he had it reprinted as an official report to Congress the following year. Lewis and Clark also prepared vocabulary lists of the Indian languages they had encountered thus far, as well as assembling for shipment samples of Indian material culture, including weapons, pottery, and buffalo robes (buffalo furs).

RAIDS AND CELEBRATIONS

The winter routine at Fort Mandan was interrupted on several occasions by dramatic events. The first occurred at the end of November, when a Mandan crossed the river from Mitutanka bringing news that Lakota Sioux and Arikara warriors had attacked a Mandan hunting party, leaving one dead, two wounded, and stealing nine of their horses. This was a grave challenge to U.S. diplomacy on the Missouri; it had only been a month since the captains had laid their prestige on the line trying to broker a peace agreement between the Arikara and the Mandan and Hidatsa tribes. Lewis and Clark decided that a show of military strength was called for, so with 21 armed men Clark set off across the frozen Missouri to offer his services to the Mandan in hunting down the Lakota Sioux and Arikara war party.

But the Mandan would have none of it. They knew better than Lewis and Clark what it meant to go chasing out over the plains through deep snow in the dead of winter. The Lakota Sioux and Arikara were well on their way home by then, and vengeance could wait until the spring. The Mandan pointed out that they had never had much faith in Arikara promises of good behavior. Clark and his men, probably a little embarrassed by the whole episode, returned to the fort.

The next time the Lakota Sioux struck it was the Americans who were their victims. On February 14 a four-man detachment from the fort, led by George Drouillard, headed south to bring in some meat killed by an earlier hunting party. They were set upon by a much larger band of Lakota Sioux (Drouillard reported there were 105 all told, although how he made such an exact count remains a mystery) who stole two of their three horses as well as a couple of knives. Such a large band of

Lakota Sioux could easily have killed the four Americans, if they had wanted to, and carried off their rifles as booty; it seems, however, that they just wanted to send a message about who really was in charge along the Missouri.

When Drouillard reported back to the fort, Lewis set out with a party of American soldiers and some Mandan warriors to attack the raiders, but after a fruitless pursuit over 30 miles of frozen landscape they gave up the chase. The captains feared renewed Lakota Sioux attack; as John Ordway noted in his journal, a French fur trader brought word that the Lakota Sioux "[s]ay if they can catch any more of us they will kill us for they think that we are bad medicine . . ." But the Americans had no more encounters with Teton Lakota Sioux that winter, and when spring came they would leave their territory far behind.

Christmas and the New Year brought happier diversions from routine. On Christmas Eve Lewis and Clark distributed flour, dried apples, and pepper—rare treats to supplement the men's usual diet of game and corn— for the next day's holiday feast. On Christmas Day, according to the account left by Private Joseph Whitehouse:

We ushred in the morning with a discharge of the Swivvel [gun], and one round of Small arms of all the party. then another from the Swivel. then Capt. Clark presented a glass of brandy to each man of the party. we hoisted the american flag, and each man had another glass of brandy. the men prepared one of the rooms and commenced dancing. at 10 oC [O'Clock] we had another Glass of brandy, at one a gun was fired as a Signal for diner. half past two another gun was fired to assemble at the dance, and So we kept it up in a jovel [jovial] manner until Eight oC [O'Clock] at night, all without the compy [company] of the female Seck [sex]. . . .

New Year's Day brought another round of celebrations. The captains ordered the cannon fired at the fort to mark the occasion. Then, at the invitation of the Mandan in Mituntaka, Clark and 16 of the expedition members, bringing a fiddle, a tambourine, and a horn, visited the village. Moving from one earthen lodge to the next, they danced with the Indians for much of the day (and some continued the celebrations through the night). The Indians "much admir'd" the men's dancing, Private Whitehouse recorded, "frequently signifying their approbation by a Whoop they gave . . ." According to Clark, the Mandan were "somewhat astonished" at York's dancing abilities, "that so large a man should be so active." (York was a source of never-ending fascination to the Indians that the Corps of Discovery encountered en route along the Pacific. On another occasion during the winter at Fort Mandan, he inadvertently helped the captains in their campaign to build better relations with one of the more aloof Hidatsa chiefs, Le Borgne. The chief, convinced that York was just a white man painted a darker color, spat on his finger and rubbed it on York's bare skin to see if the color would come off. When it did not, Le Borgne decided that the black man was Big Medicine indeed, meaning that he had powerful magical powers.)

Meanwhile, the celebration of the New Year continued. On January 2, it was Lewis's turn to take a group of soldiers over to the second Mandan village, Nuptadi, for more dancing. And from January 3 to January 5 the Mandan invited the soldiers to join them at a Buffalo Calling Dance, a ritual celebration that they believed would bring big herds of buffalo near the villages for their hunters to kill. The white men were particularly fascinated by one part of the ritual, in which hunters offered the sexual services of their wives to other men, believing that to do so would bring them luck in the hunt. Many of the young American soldiers (although apparently not Lewis and Clark themselves) eagerly took part in this part of the festivities—several months later, Clark noted in his journal that "venerials Complains" (sexually transmitted disease) was "verry Common" among the Corps' enlisted men. In any case, the ritual seemed to work; within a couple of days a herd of buffalo wandered in off the plains and furnished villagers and soldiers alike with a welcome supply of fresh meat.

GETTING READY FOR SPRING

In February Lewis and Clark began to give serious thought to their spring departure. The men chopped the boats free of the river ice that had imprisoned them since November and hauled them ashore to make repairs. At the beginning of March they cut down and began hollowing out cottonwood trees to make six dugout canoes, to replace the keelboat that Corporal Warfington would take downriver to St. Louis. By the end of March the river ice was beginning to break up. Clark was impressed by the "extraordinary dexterity" of the Indians, as they jumped from one ice floe to another and as they pulled the carcasses of drowned buffalo from the river.

Lewis and Clark resolved to be on their way westward the first week in April. They had a much better idea of what to expect along the way than they had when they arrived in October, thanks to their Mandan and Hidatsa hosts. The Indians had sketched maps of the western Missouri for them, sometimes painted onto animal skins, sometimes traced out on the earthen floors of the winter lodges. The contributions of the Hidatsa were particularly helpful, since they had traveled as far west as the Rocky Mountains. Lewis and Clark understood for the first time that the Missouri did not simply travel in a straight line west after leaving the Mandan villages. That meant that they would have more miles to travel along the actual winding course of the river than they had originally thought. Thanks to their Indian informants, it would be a lot easier for them to calculate their progress to their final goal, for they now knew the approximate distance to the various large rivers emptying into the Missouri they would find along the way. Soon after leaving the villages they would come to the Little Missouri River entering from the south, followed by the far more impressive Yellowstone River, also entering from the south. There would be two rivers entering the Missouri from the north, the White Earth River, a fairly small one, followed some days later by the only important northern tributary of the Missouri, known to the Hidatsa as The River Which Scolds at All Others. Then they would find the mouth of the Musselshell River on the south, and a few days after that they would come to the most unmistakable landmark of all, the Great Falls of the Missouri. They would have to leave the river at that point for a portage around the falls—but this detour, they were assured, was no more than a half-mile.

Once past the Great Falls the Missouri bent to the southwest. As they neared the Rocky Mountains they would come to three forks in the river. They were to take the westernmost fork, which would lead them up and over the mountains, past the headwaters of the Missouri and over the Continental Divide. On the other side, after another short portage, they would come to the headwaters of what was described to them as the south fork of the Columbia River, which would lead them to the main body of the Columbia and then to the Pacific. Clark calculated that from their portage across the Continental Divide to the Pacific would be a water journey of no more than 300 miles. He thought that meant that, with luck, they could make it to the Pacific and back to the Mandan village before the next winter set in.

There was one potential problem with this route, and that was getting across the Rockies. Even if, as they believed, it was only a few miles by land from the headwaters of the Missouri to the headwaters of the Columbia, and even if, as they also believed, the Rockies were only a few thousand feet high, the expedition still had a lot of supplies it needed to transport over the mountains, including trade goods, weapons and ammunition, cooking gear, tools, and rations. That added up to a load impossible for the men to carry on their backs. They decided that it would be necessary, once they reached the end of the Missouri's waters, to purchase horses from the Shoshone Indians, a tribe they knew lived in that region. Unlike the Mandan and Hidatsa, however, the Shoshone had never seen white men before. They spoke neither English nor French, and Lewis and Clark, of course, spoke no Shoshone. Establishing contact with the Shoshone, explaining their mission to them, and bartering for horses might prove difficult.

SACAGAWEA JOINS THE EXPEDITION

But, as fate would have it, the solution to their problem was waiting for them in one of the Hidatsa villages. For there a 47-year-old mixed-race (part French, part Indian) trader named Toussaint Charbonneau lived, along with his two Indian wives. Early in November 1804 Charbonneau came to the fort, then under construction, to see if he could interest the captains in his services as a translator. The

captains were interested, and they took him on at a salary of $25 a month. Considered on his own merits, Charbonneau did little to earn his pay; Lewis would later describe him as "a man of no particular merit," and most historians have subsequently agreed.

But Charbonneau did provide one invaluable service and that was bringing his teenage

This monument in City Park, Portland, Oregon, is a tribute to Sacagawea, shown here carrying her son. She joined the expedition as the wife of Toussaint Charbonneau and later proved indispensable to the crew as a translator among the Shoshone. She was integral to a trade for horses that made the passage across the Rockies possible. *(Library of Congress, Prints and Photographs Division [LC-USZ62-93141])*

Members of the Corps of Discovery

Captains Meriwether Lewis and
    William Clark
York, Clark's servant
Touissant Charbonneau, translator
Sacagawea, wife of Charbonneau
Jean-Baptiste Charbonneau,
    infant son of Sacagawea
    and Charbonneau
George Drouillard, interpreter
    and hunter
Sergeant Patrick Gass
Sergeant John Ordway
Sergeant Nathaniel Pryor
Private William Bratton
Private John Collins
Private John Colter
Private Pierre Cruzatte
Private Joseph Field

Private Reuben Field
Private Robert Frazer
Private George Gibson
Private Silas Goodrich
Private Hugh Hall
Private Thomas P. Howard
Private Francois Labiche
Private Baptiste Lepage
Private Hugh McNeal
Private John Potts
Private George Shannon
Private John Shields
Private John B. Thompson
Private William Werner
Private Joseph Whitehouse
Private Alexander H. Willard
Private Richard Windsor
Private Peter M. Wiser

wife Sacagawea (Sacajawea) along on the expedition (he left his older wife in the Hidatsa village). Sacagawea, whose name meant Bird Woman in Hidatsa, was about 15 years old when Lewis and Clark met her. She was a Lemhi Shoshone, born into a band that roamed a territory straddling the Continental Divide in present-day southeastern Idaho and southwestern Montana. She had not come to live among the Hidatsa by choice; five years earlier, as a girl of about 10, she had been kidnapped by Hidatsa raiders near the three forks of the Missouri River and carried back to the Knife River village as a captive. In 1803 Charbonneau acquired her as a wife, either by buying her or, according to some stories, winning her in a bet.

The captains may not have appreciated just how useful she was going to be when they

first invited Charbonneau and his young wife to move into Fort Mandan, but during the course of the winter, her participation entered more and more into their plans and calculations for the next year's journey. With Sacagawea as an unofficial part of the Corps of Discovery, when they found the Shoshone they would have a much better chance of obtaining those essential horses. Sacagawea could translate from Shoshone to Hidatsa, Charbonneau could translate the Hidatsa into French, and one of the other French speakers on the expedition could translate into English for the captains to understand. Then the chain of translation could be reversed. It would be a cumbersome system, but there were no better options available.

There was one complication: Sacagawea was pregnant, and on February 11, 1805, she went into labor. The delivery did not go well. Lewis, who handled most of the expedition's medical chores that winter, acted as her midwife. Finally, acting on the advice of René Jessaume, Lewis offered the struggling mother a drink of water with the dried rattle of a rattlesnake crumbled in it. It seemed to do the trick: Ten minutes after drinking the concoction, Sacagawea had successfully delivered her baby, a son named Jean Baptiste Charbonneau, who became better known by his nickname, "Pomp."

Sacagawea had seven weeks to regain her strength and nurse her new baby before it was time to go. At the start of April 1805, the Corps of Discovery—the party that would attempt to follow the water route to the Pacific—had taken final form. Some 40 men had sailed up the Missouri to the Mandan village in fall 1804. One, Sergeant Floyd, had died en route. A half-dozen or so French engagés had been discharged at the start of the winter. Trapper Jean-Baptiste Lepage joined up at Fort Mandan. Corporal Warfington and six soldiers (including the disgraced deserter Moses Reed and the court-martialed John Newman) would sail back on the keelboat to St. Louis, along with some of the engagés, and the interpreter Joseph Gravelines acting as pilot.

Thirty-one men, one woman and an infant, along with Lewis's big black Newfoundland Seaman, were about to sail up the unknown Missouri.

6

"THIS LITTLE FLEET"
Up the Unknown Missouri

At 4 P.M. on April 7, 1805, the Corps of Discovery proceeded on once again, this time heading up the Missouri, toward territory that no white men had ever seen. To mark the occasion, and for the first time since setting down a brief spate of journal entries in September 1804, Meriwether Lewis started making regular daily entries in his journal. Over the next few months he would be inspired to compose some of the most famous passages in the literature of exploration, including the following passage from April 7. "This little fleet," he wrote, meaning the expedition's white and red pirogues, plus the six new dugout canoes:

> altho' not quite so rispectable as those of Columbus or Capt. Cook, were still viewed by us with as much pleasure as those deservedly famed adventurers ever beheld theirs. . . . We were now about to penetrate a country at least two thousand miles in width, on which the foot of civilized man had never trodden; the good or evil it had in

store for us was for experiment yet to determine, and these little vessels contained every article by which we were to expect to subsist or defend ourselves.

Despite the uncertainty about what would befall the expedition as it headed into the unknown, Meriwether Lewis was sure of one thing: "I could but esteem this moment of my departure as among the most happy of my life."

THE JOURNEY RESUMES

Feeling the need for exercise, Lewis set out briskly on foot along the shore that afternoon while the men maneuvered the clumsy new dugouts against the Missouri's current. He walked all the way to the second Mandan village, Nuptadi, six miles from the fort, where he hoped to say goodbye to Chief Black Cat. The chief was not to be found in the village, so Lewis walked back down the river to where the expedition made its first night's encampment,

76

a mere three miles from their starting point. Next day's progress was little better, slowed by the swamping of one of the canoes, and the need to stop and dry in the sun a barrel of gunpowder that had gotten soaked.

But by the third day the expedition hit its stride, making nearly 24 miles upstream. On April 10 they made nearly 19 miles. By April 12 they had reached the first major landmark they had been told to watch for by the Hidatsa, the mouth of the Little Missouri River. During their last months on the river in 1804 they had been heading northward on the Missouri; now, coming to the section of the river that would become known as the Big Bend, they were at last heading more or less due west.

Lewis seemed pleased with everything he saw. He described the country along this stretch of the Missouri as "one continuous level fertile plain as far as the eye can reach," and a little later on as "extensive and extreemly fertile high plains and meadows." Little grew upon that "fertile plain," however, except short grass and sagebrush. Hardly a tree was to be seen past the river's edge. The farther west they traveled into the High Plains region, the drier the climate grew. Although the captains said nothing in their journals about any disagreement on the subject, Clark seemed less enchanted with the western countryside. Although his journal entries often echoed Lewis's, over the next few months adjectives like *fertile* rarely appeared in Clark's descriptions of the landscape.

Game was scarce at first because hunting parties from the Mandan and Hidatsa villages had thoroughly harvested the region during the long winter season; the expedition had traveled for four days before Drouillard and Clark finally killed a deer. Sacagawea helped fill the expedition's larder by gathering wild Jerusalem artichokes. The river also hosted an

Like buffalo, herds of pronghorn antelope provided a welcome addition to the expedition's diet. *(U.S. Fish and Wildlife Service)*

abundant population of bird life, including brant, geese, swans, gulls, ducks, and whooping cranes. When Clark killed a goose on April 13, Lewis climbed to the top of "a lofty cottonwood tree" to collect an egg from its nest, whether out of scientific curiosity or hunger for fried egg he did not say.

After five months of sedentary garrison life, the Corps of Discovery enjoyed returning to the now-familiar routine of river travel. Each morning, one of the captains would take up position as commander of the little fleet, riding in the white pirogue. The other captain—more often than not, Lewis—would

walk along the shore, often accompanied by Drouillard. After their nightly meal Cruzatte would break out his fiddle. Sometimes the men would be rewarded for a good day's progress with a dram of whiskey.

Each night Lewis and Clark would sit by the campfire and write in their journals. When it was time for bed, the captains, along with Charbonneau, Sacagawea, and Drouillard, slept in a tipi of "dressed Buffaloe skins." This was one of the few instances on the expedition in which rank obviously had its privileges; the enlisted men apparently slept in the open. Their old enemies the mosquitoes were in evi-

The Buffalo and the Plains Indian Economy

On the Corps of Discovery's return from the Pacific in 1806, Clark saw 20,000 buffalo in one day. Those numbers were far greater than the total number of all the Indians of all tribes Lewis and Clark would encounter in their two-year journey. There may have been as many as 25 million buffalo in North America then.

The ancestors of modern buffalo roamed the plains of the North American continent for hundreds of thousands of years. Human beings came along, across a temporary land bridge that spanned the Bering Strait 15 to 18 thousand years ago, and made their own way to the Plains. The Indian cultures that emerged near the buffalo came to depend on them, not only for meat, but for the hides that the Indians made into clothing and shelter, the sinews that they used for fastenings, and the bones that could be made into tools. The Indians had hunted buffalo on foot for thousands of years, stampeding them off high cliffs or past a row of archers. The introduction of the horse among the Plains Indian tribes after the 16th century greatly increased the range and effectiveness of buffalo hunters. Even so, the herds were so vast that hunting had little effect; prairie wolves, rather than human beings, were the buffalo's principal predator. Lewis was astonished at the lack of fear buffalo displayed in the presence of humans. "[T]he bull buffaloes particularly will scarcely give way to you," he wrote on May 4, 1805. "I passed several in the open plain within fifty paces, they viewed me for a moment as something novel and then very unconcernedly continued to feed."

The coming of the white hunters, with their high-powered rifles, doomed the buffalo and the Plains Indian economy that depended on the animal. By the end of the 19th century there were only about 300 adult buffalo left in all of North America.

dence early on: "I saw a Musquetor today," Clark wrote resignedly on April 9.

By the second week out, they no longer had to worry about food. "I saw Several Small parties of antelope," Clark recorded in his journal of April 17, "large herds of Elk. . . . also a Beaver house." Clark killed a buffalo and four deer while walking alone along the shore on April 21; that same day, Lewis, along with a party including Drouillard, Ordway, and Potts, accounted for three deer, two beavers, and four buffalo calves. The young buffalo, Lewis noted, were "very delicious . . . equal to any veal I ever tasted." He also wrote approvingly of the taste of beaver tail and beaver liver. The men killed for food, not for sport, and little went to waste. To feed the 33 members of the expedition, the hunters needed to bring in four deer or antelope or one buffalo every day. If they had too much fresh meat for immediate consumption, they cut the surplus into small strips and dried it, carrying it along as jerky for days when the hunters were less successful.

Through April and into May, the expedition's little fleet had to contend with high winds blowing eastward, slowing and even occasionally halting their progress. The wind

Titled *The Last of the Buffalo*, this Charles M. Russell work depicts three American Indians near a tipi. One of them is carving a buffalo horn while another smokes from a calumet and a third reclines with a bow and arrows. *(Library of Congress, Prints and Photographs Division [LC-USZ62-115204])*

severely tested the boat-handling skills of the Corps of Discovery; some were found wanting. On April 13 Touissant Charbonneau had been entrusted the helm of the white pirogue. This was the expedition's most important boat now that the keelboat was heading back to St. Louis, since it carried medicine, trade goods, and the captains' journals, as well as Sacagawea, Pomp, and several nonswimmers among the soldiers. Disaster loomed when a sudden shift in the wind's direction, followed by a miscalculation by Charbonneau at the rudder, nearly tipped the white pirogue over. With Lewis shouting orders, Drouillard seized the rudder from the hapless Charbonneau, while other men took down the sails. The boat and its precious cargo were saved.

Even when their lives were not directly endangered by it, the wind made everyone miserable. Windblown sand inflamed eyes and gummed up the works of Lewis's pocket watch: "we are compelled to eat, drink, and breathe it . . ." he complained on April 24.

WHERE NO WHITE MAN HAD BEEN BEFORE

Despite the hardships of the journey, the travelers were sustained by pride in their accomplishments. Every mile they sailed westward, they knew they were making history. On April 14, a week out from the Mandan villages, they reached a small creek running into the Missouri that they named after Charbonneau. Given that this was the same man who had nearly sunk the white pirogue the day before, it may seem strange that the captains bestowed this honor upon him. But as Lewis explained in his journal: "[W]e called [it] Sharbono's Creek, after our interpreter who encamped several weeks on it with a hunting party of Indians. this was the highest point to which any whiteman had ascended; except

two Frenchmen who having lost their way had straggled a few miles further, tho' to what place precisely I could not learn." One of the "two Frenchmen" Lewis referred to was Jean-Baptiste Lepage, who had enlisted as a member of the expedition the previous November. Lewis's account turned out to be not entirely accurate; unknown to him, another French-Canadian trader had traveled as far as the mouth of the Yellowstone River a few years earlier. But as far as Lewis knew, once the expedition had gone a few miles past Charbonneau's creek—present-day Bear Den Creek—the Corps of Discovery had entered a region that no white person had ever seen before.

On April 22 they reached the White Earth River, the first of two rivers entering the Missouri from the north that the Hidatsa had told them to expect. Lewis optimistically estimated from its appearance that its headwaters must lie deep in Canadian territory near the Saskatchewan River and that the river would be navigable most of the way there. (If true, that would have been excellent news for American fur-trading interests, but in reality the river stopped well short of the Saskatchewan region.)

On April 25, two and a half weeks after their departure, they came to a truly momentous juncture, the mouth of the Yellowstone River. Eager to get to the river, Lewis had left the little fleet behind on the Missouri that morning and hiked overland with four men and his dog, Seaman. Lewis got his first glimpse of the Yellowstone from a hilltop, which revealed "a most pleasing view of the country, particularly of the wide and fertile vallies formed by the missouri and the yellowstone rivers, which occasionally unmasked by the wood on their borders disclose their meanderings for many miles through these delightfull tracts of country." The Hidatsa had spoken glowingly of the lush Yellowstone country, of the abundance of furs waiting to be taken by trappers, and of the river's year-round navigability all the way to the foot of the Rocky Mountains. Following Jefferson's instructions, the expedition would have to stick to the Missouri River on their westward trek, but the captains had already decided to include a side trip down the Yellowstone on their return.

At noon on the next day, Clark and the rest of the expedition reached the mouth of the Yellowstone. That night the captains authorized the distribution of a dram of whisky for each man, and there was fiddle music and dancing around the campfire in celebration of reaching "this long wished for spot," as Lewis described it.

CROSSING MONTANA

Proceeding on past the mouth of the Yellowstone up the Missouri on April 27 the expedition crossed the invisible line that would be the future state border between North Dakota and Montana. Those early days in the Montana wilderness were among the most blessed in the memory of the explorers. For one thing, they were feeling very well fed. Game proved so plentiful that hunting came to resemble a shopping trip: "We can send out at any time and obtain whatever species of meat the country affords in as large quantity as we wish," Lewis wrote on May 8. Sacagawea continued to prove her value to the expedition, identifying and gathering wild edible plants along the way, like the "delicious froot," probably the Missouri or buffalo currant, that she offered to Clark on April 30.

Even in early May there were some snowy days ("a verry extraodernarey climate," Clark commented on May 2, "to behold the trees Green & flowers spred on the plain, & snow an

inch deep"). But the expedition journals also were filled with entries recording "a fine day" or "a fine morning." And, regardless of weather, the scenery was a constant delight. Lewis noted on May 4 that the "country on both sides of the Missouri continues to be open level fertile and beautifull as far as the eye can reach . . ." Clark, as usual, dropped the "fertile," but conceded in his own entry for that day that the countryside was "rich high and butifull . . ."

The expedition continued to make good progress up the Missouri. The Hidatsa had told them they would encounter a major river entering the Missouri from the north, The River Which Scolds at All Others, about 500 miles to the west of the Mandan villages. Sure enough, on May 8, a month and a day after their departure, they came across its mouth. Finding the Indian name too much of a mouthful, they renamed it the Milk River. Lewis was once again hopeful that the Milk "might furnish a practicable and advantageous communication with the Saskaashiwan river" and the rich fur-trapping region around it (and, once again, as at the White Earth River, he proved mistaken).

As the Missouri began to cut a deeper channel through the surrounding countryside, its high, crumbling riverbanks posed a new threat to the expedition. "I sometimes wonder," Lewis wrote on May 11, "that some of our canoes or perogues are not swallowed up by means of the immence mass of earth which are eternally precipitating themselves into the river."

But human error proved more dangerous than nature. Once again Charbonneau had been allowed to take the rudder of the white pirogue, and once again he proved unfit. On May 14 a sudden squall caught the little fleet unaware. Lewis and Clark were both on shore, violating their usual rule that one of them

Encounters with a Grizzly

Montana's abundant wildlife included one new creature whose acquaintance the Corps of Discovery would have preferred not to have made: the grizzly bear. The Mandan had warned the corps of the grizzly's fierceness. They never hunted for the bears unless they had six or more warriors along. Despite this warning, Lewis and Clark tended to discount the grizzly's fierce reputation. Lewis and another hunter killed a young male grizzly on April 29. Although it took three shots to bring the bear down, Lewis wrote complacently in his journal that night: "The Indians may well fear this anamal, equipped as they generally are with their bows and arrows, but in the hands of skillful riflemen they are by no means as formidable or dangerous as they have been represented."

On May 5 Clark and Drouillard encountered another grizzly, "a very large and turrible looking animal, which we found verry hard to kill" according to Clark. It took 10 musket balls, five of them in the lungs, to bring the beast down. When they measured it afterward, they found that the bear stood well over eight feet tall and had nearly five-inch-long talons; they estimated that it weighed more than five hundred pounds. Lewis adopted a more respectful tone in his journal: "I find that the curiousity of our party is pretty well satis-fyed with rispect to this anamal." They may have been done with grizzlies, but grizzlies were not done with them. On the late afternoon of May 11 Private Bratton encountered a bear along the shore and shot him through the lungs; severely wounded as he was, the bear then pursued Bratton for half a mile before giving up the chase. Lewis sent a party out to finish off the wounded grizzly and confessed in his journal pages that he would "reather fight two Indians than one bear."

should remain aboard the white pirogue. Seeing it turned broadside to the wind and beginning to take on water, all they could do was yell desperately from the shore for Charbonneau to come about, or turn the boat. As Lewis wrote disgustedly in his journal that night: "Charbono, still crying to his god for mercy, had not yet recollected the rudder, nor could the repeated orders of the bowsman, Cruzat, bring him to his recollection untill he threatened to shoot him instantly if he did not take hold of the rudder and do his duty . . ." Cruzatte's threat worked; Charbonneau finally grabbed the rudder and turned the boat into the wind. The men bailed the water with cooking pots, and the pirogue was saved.

Though Charbonneau disgraced himself, his wife impressed the men of the Corps of Discovery with her coolheaded competence. Even Lewis, who did not yet seem to hold Sacagawea in high regard, wrote warmly of her performance that day: "The Indian woman, to whom I ascribe equal fortitude and resolution with any person on board at the time of the accident, caught and preserved most of the light articles, which were washed overboard." Her actions were all the more remarkable, considering she had to keep her

When Lewis and Clark made their journey, there may have been more than 100,000 grizzly bears roaming the area that was destined to become the lower 48 states of the United States. Today there are perhaps 1,100 left, most of them on national parkland in Montana and Wyoming.

Seemingly calm and approachable in the photograph, the grizzly bear is actually a fierce animal that can run up to 35 miles per hour and weigh up to 1,500 pounds. *(National Park Service)*

infant son, Pomp, safe. At camp that night the captains had a ration of whiskey from their dwindling supply distributed to the men to calm everybody's nerves—probably including their own.

Although the men often had to jump into the river or scramble along the sharp stones and slippery mud of the riverbank in order to pull the boats through shallow or rapid stretches with towropes, they made continued progress. On May 20 the Corps of Discovery reached the Musselshell River, another of the landmarks they had been told to look for. On May 29 they came to the mouth of a river entering the Missouri from the south that had gone unmentioned by the Hidatsa. Clark took the opportunity to name it Judith's River, after Julia (Judith) Hancock, a young girl he knew back home. After his return from the expedition, Julia, by then aged 16, became his wife; her river would in time become known as the Judith River, without the apostrophe and *s*.

SPECTACULAR LANDSCAPE

Starting in the third week of May, snow-capped mountains began appearing on the horizon. On May 17 Clark spotted some high peaks to the north of the river, westward from their position: They were part of the Little Rocky Mountains, an outlying range detached from and well east of the Rockies. On May 25 Clark noted more mountains to both the north and south of the Missouri: these were the Little Rocky and Bears Paw ranges to the north and the Judith range to the south. Clark understood that these mountains were not the long-sought Rockies described to them by the Hidatsa. But in the distance, farther to the southwest, he saw another "range of high mounts." Although Clark did not speculate in his journal as to the identity of those high mounts, Lewis saw them the next day and instantly decided they must be the Rockies. He confessed to his journal his "secret pleasure" in arriving "so near the head of heretofore conceived boundless Missouri . . ." (In reality, the peaks hovering tantalizingly on the southwest horizon were probably the Highwood Mountains, still another detached range, and not part of the Rockies.) Lewis's pleasure in viewing the mountains was not unmixed; he

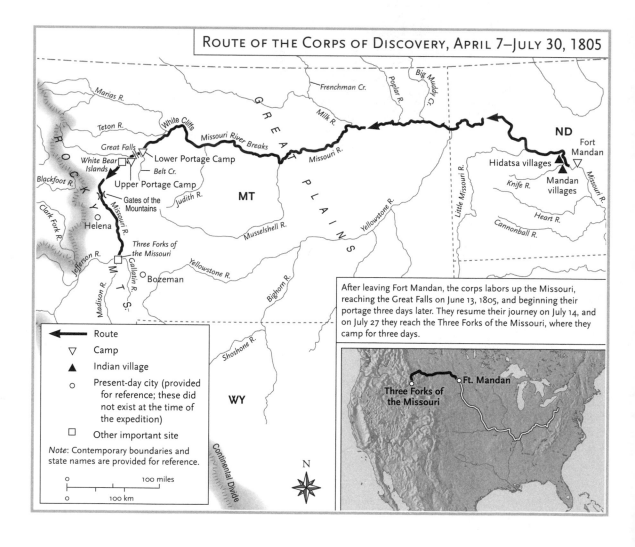

ROUTE OF THE CORPS OF DISCOVERY, APRIL 7–JULY 30, 1805

Route

▽ Camp

▲ Indian village

o Present-day city (provided for reference; these did not exist at the time of the expedition)

□ Other important site

Note: Contemporary boundaries and state names are provided for reference.

100 miles

100 km

After leaving Fort Mandan, the corps labors up the Missouri, reaching the Great Falls on June 13, 1805, and beginning their portage three days later. They resume their journey on July 14, and on July 27 they reach the Three Forks of the Missouri, where they camp for three days.

Three Forks of the Missouri

Ft. Mandan

confessed to some worries about the "sufferings and hardship" that "this snowey barrier would most probably throw in my way to the Pacific. . . ." But he concluded on a more optimistic note: "I will believe it a good comfortable road untill I am compelled to believe differently."

The mountains were spectacular but distant. Closer at hand, the hills and bluffs that now lined the river provided some of the most wondrous scenery the expedition had yet encountered. They were entering the section of the river later designated the Missouri Breaks. In the White Cliffs area of the Missouri Breaks, the river had cut deeply through surrounding layers of shale and sandstone. The towering cliffs that resulted on either side of the river had eroded over hundreds of thousands of years into fantastic shapes that seemed, especially to someone with a romantic temperament like Meriwether Lewis, a kind of dream landscape. In his journal entry for May 31, Lewis described that day's journey as having passed through scenes "of visionary enchantment." In another of the justifiably famous journal entries he made that spring, Lewis wrote of the White Cliffs:

> The water in the course of time in decending from those hills and plains on either side of the river has trickled down the soft sand cliffs and woarn it into a thousand grotesque figures, which with the help of a little immagination and an oblique view, at a distance are made to represent eligant ranges of lofty freestone buildings, having their parapets well stocked with statuary; collumns of various sculptures both grooved and plain, are also seen supporting long galleries in front of those buildings; in other places on a much nearer approach and with the help of less immagination we see the remains of ruins of eligant build-

ings; some collumns standing and almost entire with their pedestals and capitals; others retaining their pedestals but deprived by time or accident of their capitals, some lying prostrate and broken othe[r]s in the form of vast pyramids of connic structure bearing a sereis of other pyramids on their tops becoming less as they ascend and finally terminating in a sharp point.

On June 2, still within the Missouri Breaks, they came to the mouth of another unexpected river. This one posed a problem more difficult than what to name it because, unlike the Judith, it entered the Missouri from the north. From what the Hidatsa had told Lewis and Clark the previous winter, or at least from what they had understood them to say, the expedition should already have passed the last major northern tributary of the Missouri, the River Which Scolds at All Others, which they had renamed the Milk. Was this then the real Scolding River, or another river entirely? Or was it a fork in the Missouri that had also gone unmentioned—and if so, which fork was the one that would lead them to the Rockies?

In reality they had stumbled across an entirely separate river—and not a very impressive river at that. Had it not been swollen by spring rains upstream, they never would have been mistaken it for a fork of the mighty Missouri. But the captains needed to make sure. From June 3 through June 12 the expedition camped at the junction of the two rivers, at a place later known as Decision Point.

Already by the afternoon of June 3, Lewis and Clark had a strong hunch that the southern "fork" was the real Missouri. The northern river was muddier than the southern, and the captains reasoned that it had gotten that way by running a long way through open plains. The southern river being clearer, it seemed more likely that it flowed a relatively shorter distance out of the mountains, and was thus the river they wanted to follow. But most of the enlisted men were not persuaded by the captains' argument, and that included men whose opinions about rivers were worth taking seriously, like the experienced boatman Cruzatte.

Taking the wrong fork now would mean delay or even worse. To "mistake the stream at this period of the season . . ." Lewis wrote in his journal on June 3, "and to ascend such stream to the rocky Mountain or perhaps much further before we could inform ourselves whether it did approach the Columbia or not, and then be obliged to return and take the other stream would not only loose us the whole of the season but would probably so dishearten the party that it might defeat the expedition altogether." The fate of the Corps of Discovery rested on the decision Lewis and Clark would now make.

7

To the Missouri Headwaters

The Corps of Discovery faced a serious choice and would have to make sure they were right before they could proceed any further. Clark led a party up the southern river far enough to spot more snow-capped mountains in the distance (the Little Belt and Big Belt ranges) and to determine that the river was heading in the southwesterly direction predicted by the Hidatsa. Returning to Decision Point, he felt reassured that he and Lewis were right in saying that the southern river was, in fact, the true Missouri. Lewis, meanwhile, led a party 40 miles up the northern river; although it headed west from its juncture with the Missouri it soon bent northward. Lewis was now equally certain that he and Clark had been right in their earlier hunch and that this was not the Missouri. Lewis named the northern river Maria's River after his cousin Maria Wood—like the Judith, the name would evolve and eventually lose the possessive apostrophe, becoming the Marias River.

Lewis and Clark rendezvoused at Decision Point on June 8. Although they were certain in their own minds as to how to proceed, their men remained unconvinced. Lewis could have ordered them back into the boats to follow his and Clark's lead, as was his right as commander. But he decided that it was more important for everyone to be in agreement on their course, even at the cost of a few more days' delay. If he could find the Great Falls of the Missouri along the southern river, there could no longer be any question as to the direction they should follow.

THE GREAT FALLS OF THE MISSOURI

On June 11 Lewis set out up the southern river, accompanied by Drouillard and three others. He had been suffering from violent stomach cramps and a fever for several days and it slowed his progress. That night, he had his

This etching of Clark shooting grizzly bears suggests the animals were a dangerous foe. *(Library of Congress, Prints and Photographs Division [LC-USZ62-19233])*

men brew up a medicinal concoction of boiled chokecherry twigs, a legacy of his mother's herbal lore. He swallowed the brew, and it seemed to work.

Setting out the next day with renewed vigor, Lewis and his men made 27 miles up the Missouri. On the morning of June 13, walking along the prairie, high above the river, Lewis spotted what looked like smoke in the distance, and he heard a deep roaring noise. He was seeing the spray and hearing the sound of falling waters. Seven miles farther on, a "sublimely grand specticle" awaited the explorers as they peered down from the prairie's edge at the Great Falls, an 80-foot precipice, 300 yards wide, that sent a vast flow of water crashing down to the river bottom. Lewis climbed down from the prairie's edge to the foot of the falls. For the

next four hours he sat transfixed by the scene, "the grandest sight I ever beheld."

The next day Joseph Field set off, carrying a letter from Lewis to Clark reporting on the discovery. Lewis, meanwhile, headed back up to the high ground to scout out the portage that lay ahead. He soon discovered that the "Great Falls" was not singular at all, as they had thought, but plural: five sets of falls altogether, stretching over 10 miles of river. The scenery was grand, to be sure, but the trip around the falls would require a much longer portage than their conversations with their Hidatsa friends the previous winter had prepared them to expect. The water route to the Pacific was taking on unexpected complications.

Lewis's adventures were not over for the day. Deciding to postpone his return to the

The Many Names of Sacagawea ⌒

Lewis and Clark's journals reveal the captains' growing appreciation for Sacagawea. The ways in which they chose to refer to her between 1804 and the end of 1805 are very revealing. When they first encountered her at Fort Mandan she was known to them only as one of Toussaint Charbonneau's two "Squars," or squaws. When Lewis helped deliver her baby in February 1805, he referred to her as "one of the wives of Charbono . . ." They had decided to take her along on their trip hoping she would serve as an interpreter to the Shoshone, but her status did not improve: She was still only a nameless wife when Lewis recorded her as a member of the group departing Fort Mandan on April 5, 1805: "an Indian woman wife to Charbono . . ."

Six weeks later she finally got a name. By then she had proven her usefulness to the expedition as a forager of new and interesting foods, like the Jerusalem artichokes she dug up for their meal on April 9. And then, when

Charbonneau nearly overturned the pirogue on May 14, she had helped save the expedition's supplies from the Missouri's waters. She earned the captains' respect, and as a token of their appreciation they decided to bestow her name on one of the rivers they came upon entering into the Missouri: "This stream," Lewis wrote on May 20, "we call Sah-ca-gar me ah or bird woman's River, after our interpreter the Snake* [Shoshone] woman."

(continues)

As the trip progressed, Lewis and Clark's appreciation for Sacagawea grew. This statue in Great Falls, Montana, commemorates the three and Sacagawea's presence as their right-hand woman.
(Bureau of Land Management)

---

* Traders in the area often collectively called the Northern Shoshone, Northern Paiute (Numu), and Bannock the Snake. Writings done at that time on Sacagawea often refer to her as Snake.

(continued)

By November she had earned an affectionate nickname as well, at least as far as Clark was concerned. The men were debating where they should make their winter camp. "Janey in favour of a place where there is plenty of Potas [potatoes—meaning camas root here]," Clark recorded in his journal on November 24. And so the young Indian woman had progressed from nameless "squar" to "Sacagawea" to "Janey" in her first year in the company of the Corps of Discovery.

camp at the lower falls, he shot a buffalo for his supper. But as he approached his fallen prey with a now empty gun, he spotted a grizzly heading straight for him. Lewis started to retreat, and the grizzly kept on coming. Lewis had his espontoon, his spear-pointed walking stick, with him, but he knew would do him little good in face-to-face combat with a giant grizzly. In desperation, he waded waist-deep into the Missouri and turned to face his adversary. This time it was the bear that flinched; it turned and fled. Reloading his rifle (and vowing never to neglect that precaution again), Lewis went back to reclaim the dead buffalo. But then he saw another fearsome-looking creature of the "tiger kind" (possibly a wolverine) looking as though it intended to spring at him; he fired at it and it disappeared down its burrow.

Having decided that "all the beasts of the neighborhood had made a league to distroy me," Lewis abandoned any notion of spending a night alone on the prairie and set off for home, although not before three buffalo bulls charged him (changing their minds, Lewis believed, when they got close enough to him to see that he was not likely to be stampeded by their bravado). These "curious adventures" seemed to Lewis like something out of a tale of "inchantment"; he thought it

all "might be a dream," but he was reminded that he was awake and had a long way still to walk by the prickly pear spines "which pierced my feet very severely. . . ." He finally arrived back at camp long after dark, to the relief of his men, who had become concerned. But his encounters with the animal kingdom were not quite over; upon awakening the next day, he found that a large rattlesnake lay curled up 10 feet away from where he was sleeping.

Meanwhile, on June 12, Clark and the rest of the men had set out up the Missouri after making a cache of supplies to recover on their return trip. In two pits, they left a half-ton of food, gunpowder, tools, weapons, and other supplies. They also left behind the red pirogue, camouflaged beneath a pile of brush on a small wooded island near Decision Point. As they set out upriver, Clark fretted about Sacagawea's health. She had been very sick for several days from an unknown ailment, feverish and suffering stomach pain, and although he had several times opened a vein on her arm and let a considerable portion of blood drain out before tying off the wound (a common medical practice of the era, which supposedly helped purify "bad blood"), she did not seem any the better for it. "The Interpreters woman verry Sick worse than she has been," Clark noted in his journal on the evening of June 12.

On June 14 Joseph Field came down the river and delivered to Clark the note from Lewis announcing the discovery of Great Falls. He also warned Clark that for several miles below the falls, the river ran too rapidly to allow for safe passage of the boats. On June 15 the main party with Clark camped about a mile below a side stream that Field had said might be used as a path to exit from the Missouri for their portage. Lewis and his party joined them at their riverside camp the next day.

THE PORTAGE

Lewis told Clark what he had seen upriver. He recommended that they follow a portage route along the river's south side. Clark agreed, and they moved their camp to the small stream entering on the south side of the river that they called Portage Creek (present-day Belt Creek). The camp they set up here would be known as Lower Portage Camp. While Clark set out to reconnoiter the portage route, Lewis took over the task of treating Sacagawea's illness; it would be a disaster if she died, he wrote, not only for her own sake, but because she was "our only dependence for a friendly negociation with the Snake [Shoshone] Indians on whom we depend for horses to assist us in our portage from the Missouri to the columbia river." He gave her a dose of powdered bark and opium and also had her drink mineral water from a local spring, which seemed to work better than Clark's bleedings. Within a few days she showed definite signs of recovery.

Lewis meanwhile oversaw preparations for the portage. They would leave the white pirogue hidden near the Lower Portage Camp for their return trip, along with another cache of supplies. He put the men to work constructing wooden carts, which they would use to drag the expedition's supplies and canoes across the prairie portage. Clark returned on June 20, suggesting they make their upper camp past the mouth of the Medicine River, near what he called White Bears Island (named for the grizzlies that inhabited it). He estimated the distance between the two camps at 17 3/4 miles.

They set out on the portage on June 22. Lewis directed that the iron frame of his experimental boat, which they had hauled all the way from Harpers Ferry in Virginia, be included in the first load. While most of the party under Clark would cross and recross the route between Lower Portage camp and White Bears Island camp, Lewis and a smaller group would remain at the upper camp to assemble the iron boat. When completed, it would take the place of the white pirogue they had left below.

If the men had thought that towing the pirogues and canoes up the Missouri's waters was hard work, they now found themselves engaged in even more strenuous labor. The portage route was over rough ground, frequently cut by deep ravines. The little hand-made carts were hard to push or control; they broke down and had to be repaired. Prickly pear cactus spines cut through moccasins and punctured feet. The men endured storms that dropped hailstones the size of apples that left them with bloody heads. On a side trip to view the Great Falls, Clark, Charbonneau, Sacagawea, and Pomp were caught in a terrible summer downpour; sheltering in a ravine, they were almost swept away in a flash flood. The Corps of Discovery stumbled on, bleeding and exhausted: "[A]t every halt," Lewis wrote, "these poor fellows tumble down and are so

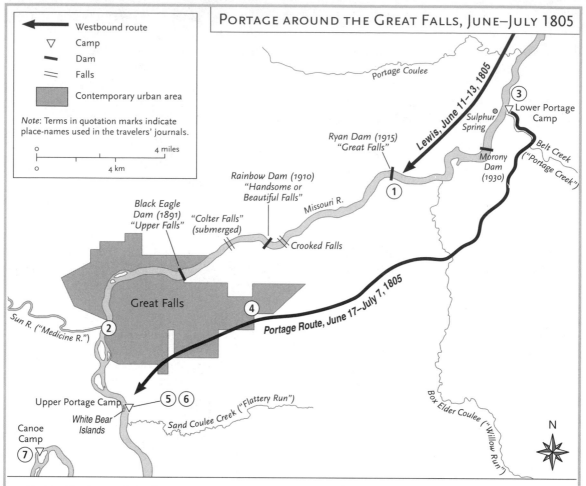

PORTAGE AROUND THE GREAT FALLS, JUNE–JULY 1805

Westbound route
▽ Camp
▬ Dam
= Falls

Contemporary urban area

Note: Terms in quotation marks indicate place-names used in the travelers' journals.

0   4 miles
0   4 km

Portage Coulee

Lewis, June 11–13, 1805

③ Lower Portage Camp

Sulphur Spring

Ryan Dam (1915) "Great Falls"

Morony Dam (1930)

Belt Creek ("Portage Creek")

①

Rainbow Dam (1910) "Handsome or Beautiful Falls"

Missouri R.

Black Eagle Dam (1891) "Upper Falls"

"Colter Falls" (submerged)

Crooked Falls

Great Falls

④

Portage Route, June 17–July 7, 1805

Sun R. ("Medicine R.")

②

Box Elder Coulee ("Willow Run")

Upper Portage Camp

⑤ ⑥

White Bear Islands

Sand Coulee Creek ("Flattery Run")

Canoe Camp

⑦ ▽

N

1. "I wished for the pencil of Salvator Rosa, a Titian, or the pen of Thomson, that I might be enabled to give to the enlightened world some just idea of this truly magnificent and sublimely grand object which has, from the commencement of time, been concealed from the view of civilized man."
   —Meriwether Lewis, June 13, 1805

2. ". . . a large white, or reather brown bear had perceived and crept on me within twenty steps before I discovered him. In the first moment I drew up my gun to shoot, but at the same instant recolected that she was not loaded . . ."
   —Meriwether Lewis, June 14, 1805

3. "The Indian woman verry bad, & will take no medisin what ever . . . If she dies it will be the fault of her husband as I am now convinced."
   —William Clark, June 16, 1805

4. "At every halt these poor fellos tumble down and are so much fortiegued that many of them are asleep in an

instant. In short, their fatiegues are incredible . . . yet no one complains. All go with cheerfullness."
   —Meriwether Lewis, June 23, 1805

5. "It being the 4th of Independence we drank the last of our ardent Spirits except a little reserved for Sickness."
   —John Ordway, July 4, 1805

6. "Therefore for want of tar or pitch we had, after all our labour, to haul our new [iron-frame] boat on shore, and leave it at this place."
   —Patrick Gass, July 9, 1805

7. "About 11 o'clock we set out from this place, which we had called Canoe Camp."
   —Patrick Gass, July 15, 1805

Note: Original spelling and punctuation have been retained from journal entries.

much fortiegued that many of them are asleep in an instant."

Meanwhile, work went on at the upper camp assembling Lewis's experimental boat. Wood had to be cut and shaped to fill out the frame; animal skins had to be prepared and sewn together to serve as the boat's hull. Lewis took on the job of camp cook, preparing buffalo dumplings as a special treat for his hard-working men.

On July 2, Clark and his weary men delivered the last load of supplies. The boat was not yet finished, so the men who were not working on it got a few days' rest. On July 4 they celebrated Independence Day with the last of the expedition's whisky. Lewis and Clark meanwhile had quietly decided that they would not, as originally intended, send anyone back from the Great Falls to report to Jefferson on the expedition's progress. They were going to need every man they had for the challenges to come. They also now realized it would be impossible for the Corps of Discovery to reach the Pacific and return to Fort Mandan for its winter encampment that year as previously planned. If they made it to the Pacific in 1805, that would be where they would have to spend the winter.

The iron boat was completed and ready for a trial sailing on July 9. It leaked. Lewis had counted on sealing the seams of the sewn animal skins with a tar made from pine pitch, but no pines grew at the Great Falls. The mixture of charcoal and tallow that Lewis devised as a substitute did not work. They had lugged the iron frame across two-thirds of the North American continent for nothing. "I need not add that this circumstance mortifyed me not a little," Lewis wrote in his journal. "I bid a dieu to my boat. . . ." The failure of Lewis's cherished experiment meant there would be still further delay in setting off. To take the place of the iron boat, they had to build two more dugout canoes, costing them five more summer travel days.

CLOSING IN ON THE ROCKIES

On July 15 the expedition once again proceeded on up the Missouri. Ahead of them they could see the Rockies—the real Rockies this time—in the distance. The men were distributed among the eight dugout canoes. They were, for the first time, traveling without any of their original fleet: The white pirogue was cached at Lower Portage Camp, the red pirogue further back at Decision Point, and the keelboat under the command of Corporal Warfington had reached St. Louis on May 20. The river was changing direction again. West of Great Falls the Missouri bent south, just as the Hidatsa had told them it would.

On July 16, they found hoofprints and willow shelters along the riverside. An Indian party had camped there. Although they judged the signs of Indian presence as being at least a week and a half old, it was the closest they had come to encountering other human beings since shortly after their departure from the Mandan villages. Looking at the abandoned camp, Sacagawea thought its inhabitants must have been from her own tribe, the Shoshone.

These were the Indians Lewis and Clark most wanted to meet. But they were not going to catch up with a party of mounted Shoshone while traveling up the river in the dugout canoes. They also feared that the sound of gunfire from their hunters' rifles would spook the Shoshone, who might fear the shots came from a Hidatsa raiding party. So on July 18 Clark, accompanied by Joseph Field, John Potts, and York, headed out overland as an advance party searching for the Shoshone, while Lewis remained behind in command of the expedition fleet.

On July 19 Lewis's little fleet reached a narrow rocky gorge cut by the Missouri through the Big Belt mountain range, "the most remarkable clifts we have yet seen." He named the entrance to the gorge "the Gates of the Rocky Mountains." The river twisted and turned through nearly six miles of high cliffs on either side, before reentering the plains. Clark's party rejoined the expedition on the Missouri on July 21, without having encountered any Shoshone (although they did observe the smoke of a distant prairie fire, started perhaps by Indians to warn others of the presence of the strangers coming up the Missouri). Clark's report was disappointing, but Sacagawea gave them reason for optimism. Lewis noted in his journal: "The Indian woman recognizes the country and assures us that this is the river on which her relations live, and that the three forks are at no great distance. this peice of information has cheered the sperits of the party, who now begin to console themselves with the anticipation of shortly seeing the head of the missouri, yet unknown to the civilized world."

THREE FORKS

The Three Forks of the Missouri were nearby, just as Sacagawea promised. Clark set out to find them on July 23, heading overland again with a small party consisting of Joseph and Reuben Field, Robert Frazer, and Charbonneau. Despite Clark's badly bruised feet, they hiked 23 miles that first day; 30 the next. On the third day out, the morning of July 25, they reached the forks. Here, 2,464 miles from its mouth on the Mississippi, the mighty Missouri divided into three clear and fast-running streams, all running over clean bottoms of smooth pebbles and gravel. It was a remark-

ably beautiful spot, with mountains visible to the east, west, and south (later to be named the Bridger range, the Tobacco Root Mountains, and the Jefferson, Madison and Gallatin ranges stretching before them on the vista from southwest to southeast).

To Clark, it was obvious at a glance that the westernmost fork of the Missouri was the most substantial of the three and that it led most directly to the mountains they sought. He saw signs that Indians had passed through the area within the past week, but none were to be found there that day. Clark left a message for Lewis attached to a pole, and headed up the western fork to see what he could learn about the river's course.

Lewis arrived with the remainder of the party at the Three Forks two days later. Sacagawea was with him. She had now traveled

As U.S. secretary of the treasury, Albert Gallatin was a strong supporter of the Lewis and Clark expedition. *(Library of Congress, Prints and Photographs Division [LC-USZ62-110017])*

full circle back to the place of her kidnapping five years before by the Hidatsa. Lewis watched Sacagawea curiously. He wanted to see how she would react to finding herself again on home territory, but professed himself disappointed at her apparent indifference: "I cannot discover that she shews any immotion of sorrow in recollecting this event," he wrote, "or of joy in being again restored to her native country; if she has enough to eat and a few trinkets to wear I believe she would be perfectly content anywhere." Lewis's assumptions about Sacagawea's inner feelings are a reminder that he may have been a better interpreter of the natural world than he was of the emotions of other human beings. Sacagawea had been through a lot in her young life; displays of emotion had rarely won her any advantage, so it is not surprising that, if she felt any great happiness at being back at Three Forks, she kept those feelings to herself.

Clark and his men limped down to Three Forks on the afternoon of July 27 and rejoined the main party. The captains decided they should remain there for two days and give the men a chance to recuperate from the heavy exertions of recent weeks. They named the "three noble streams" that diverged at Three Forks after their country's leaders: the westernmost—and from their perspective, most important—branch would be the Jefferson, the middle branch would be the Madison (named for Secretary of State James Madison) and the easternmost branch would be the Gallatin (named for Secretary of the Treasury Albert Gallatin).

SEARCHING FOR THE SHOSHONE

In their homes back east, in Virginia and Kentucky, late July was the height of summer. In western Montana, however, it was a time when winter's approach could first be detected in the air. The days were hot, but the nights were getting cold. Game was beginning to get scarce as well. And there were no Shoshone or their horses to be seen. Though he did not share his worries with his men, Lewis confided to his journal in an entry on July 27 that "we begin to feel considerable anxiety with rispect to the Snake [Shoshone] Indians. if we do not find them or some other nation who have horses I fear the successfull issue of our voyage will be very doubtfull. . . ."

There was nothing to do but press on and hope that the next day or the next bend in the river would finally lead them to the Shoshone. On July 30 the Corps of Discovery set out up the newly named Jefferson River, Clark in a dugout canoe and Lewis on foot, walking along the riverbank with Charbonneau and his wife. Sacagawea pointed out to Lewis the precise spot from which she had been captured by the Hidatsa five years earlier.

Still no Shoshone, and the canoes were making slow progress. The river was no longer really navigable; most of the time the men had to wade upstream dragging the canoes over the shallow, stony river bottom. Lewis decided to push on ahead overland. On August 1 he set out with Drouillard, Charbonneau, and Gass. On August 4 they came to another fork in the river. This time Lewis judged that the more easterly or left fork, not the westernmost or right fork, to be the one that came down most directly from the mountains, judging by the flow and color of the water. This easterly fork would later become known as the Beaverhead River. Lewis left a note on a pole for Clark telling him to follow this fork.

To make sure he had chosen correctly, however, Lewis decided to reconnoiter the right, or westerly fork (present-day Big Hole River).

The Rocky Mountains

Lewis and Clark had long hoped and feared the day they would arrive at the foot of the Rocky Mountains, "this snowey barrier," as Lewis called it. As European geographers realized early on, the Rockies were among the most significant features of the North American landscape, a formidable barrier between the Great Plains of central North America and the land that reached to the Pacific. Passing through and over the Rockies would prove the most difficult challenge faced by Lewis and Clark on their expedition.

The Rocky Mountains are an interlocking chain of more than 20 ranges and groups of mountains that extend more than 3,000 miles from New Mexico to Canada and Alaska. In places, the Rocky Mountains are more than 350 miles wide, with individual peaks ranging in height from 7,000 feet to more than 14,000 feet. The Rockies form the line of the Continental Divide. From the eastern flanks of the Rocky Mountains, water flows toward the Atlantic; from the Rockies' western flanks, water flows to the Pacific. Those rivers with headwaters in the Rockies whose waters ultimately flow to the Atlantic include the Missouri, Yellowstone, Rio Grande, Arkansas, Platte, and Saskatchewan Rivers. Those rivers with headwaters in the Rockies whose waters ultimately flow to the Pacific include the Columbia, Colorado, Snake, Fraser and Yukon Rivers. In Canada, the Peace, Athabasca, and Liard Rivers flow from the Rockies northward to the Arctic Ocean.

The Rockies were created by a complex succession of geological movements over a period of tens of million years. Geologists call the process that created the Rockies the Laramide Orogeny (*orogeny* is a technical term geologists use for "mountain building"; "Laramide" refers to the Laramie Mountains of eastern Wyoming, where the geological process that created the Rockies was first identified). The Rockies' geological origins can be found in the eastward shifting of the earth's plates under the Pacific Ocean, a process whose technical name is *plate tectonics*. The plates that underlie the earth's surface move and collide with one another; the plate underlying the Pacific Ocean collided with the plate that lay under the North American continent tens of millions of years ago. The collision between two tectonic plates is the underlying cause of the formation of both the Rocky Mountains and the Appalachian Mountains, although there are some important differences that help to explain why the two ranges look so different. First, the collision of the plates related to the uplift of the Rockies occurred much more recently than the collision that created the predecessors of the Appalachian Mountains. Second, the collision related to the Rockies was not between two slabs of continental crust but between oceanic crust and continental crust.

The Laramide Orogeny, the name given to the mountain-building event that created the present-day Rocky Mountains, started in the Late Cretaceous (80 million years ago) with the subduction of the oceanic Pacific Plate (and related plates) under the North American plate. The makeup of the plates is important for understanding the types of mountains that were formed. The less dense continental crust overrode the denser basaltic oceanic crust of the Pacific plate. As the rocks of the Pacific plate were pushed down into the mantle, some of the material carried along with the plate started melting. The partially molten material moved upward toward the surface and formed igneous rocks—volcanic rock, if it emerged on the surface; intrusive rock, like granite, if it cooled below the surface.

The collision of the two plates occurred at a relatively high speed (10 centimeters/year), which produced a great deal of crustal deformation in a belt stretching from present-day western Idaho to central Montana. The deformation (mountain-building) included folding and thrusting of existing sedimentary rocks on the western side of the deformed zone (the mountain ranges of western Montana and Wyoming, eastern Idaho, and eastern Utah), crystalline-cored uplifts in the east (mountains of south-central Montana, central and eastern Wyoming, and central Colorado), intrusive igneous ranges (mountains like the Bitterroot Range, which were such an obstacle to Lewis and Clark), and extrusive igneous ranges (the volcanic rocks of Montana and Wyoming). The overall mountain ranges that resulted from the first part of this tectonic event probably looked somewhat like the Andes, with a narrow coastal zone receiving sediment from high eroding mountains.

About 50 million years ago, the plate movement changed so that the Pacific plate started moving more northerly (instead of northeast or east), and the rate of convergence slowed. This had an effect like a plow backing up—the thrusted and uplifted mountain ranges sagged down. This also caused the "magmatic arc" (the zone of partially melted crust associated with the subducted plate) to "sweep" back toward the northwest, resulting in another round of igneous intrusion and volcanism. Younger mountain ranges in central Montana and Wyoming, such as the Bearpaws, the Highwood, and the Crazies were formed during this round of the orogeny.

At about 17.5 million years ago, the movement of the plate became more northwesterly. This change in motion created tears in the continental crust that trended in a roughly east-west direction, and igneous features such as the Columbia River Plateau and the Snake River Plain started forming. In geological terms, the history of the Rockies is all part of the earth's recent past. Unlike the ancient mountains of the eastern United States, the Rocky Mountains may still be growing.

Geographers today divide the Rocky Mountains into five sections. The Southern Rockies, found in New Mexico, Colorado and southern Wyoming, include the Laramie, Medicine Bow, Sangre de Cristo, and San Juan Mountains, as well as the Front Range of the Rockies. Many of the peaks in the southern Rockies rise

(continues)

(continued)

to more than 14,000 feet, including Mt. Elbert, in the Sawatch Mountains, at 14,433 feet the highest of all the Rockies. The southern Rockies were the first to be approached by European explorers. The city of Santa Fe, founded by the Spanish in 1598 in present-day New Mexico, was for centuries the northernmost outpost of the Spanish Empire in North America; it lies on the southwest flank on the Sangre de Cristo Mountains. In the 19th century the Front Range of the Rockies, running 300 miles northward of Pikes Peak in Colorado, would attract the attention of such famous American explorers as Zebulon Pike (for whom Pikes Peak was named), Stephen Long (who gave his name to Longs Peak), and John Wesley Powell (the first explorer to sail the Colorado River through the length of the Grand Canyon).

The Middle Rockies lie in northwestern Colorado, northeastern Utah, and western Wyoming and include the Teton Range (destined to become a favorite destination for generations of American mountaineers), as well as the Big Horn, Beartooth, Owl Creek Uinta, and Wind River Mountains. The Wind River range is pierced by South Pass, first discovered in 1812 by fur trader and explorer Robert Stuart, a 25-mile-wide opening through the mountains that rises gradually to a height of 7,550 feet. Unlike other Rocky Mountain passes, South Pass offered abundant water and grass along the way and would in time prove accessible to wagons pulled by teams of horses or oxen. For that reason, in years to come the relatively easy access across the Rockies offered by South Pass would become a crucial element in the Oregon Trail.

The Northern Rockies are the section that Lewis and Clark encountered in 1805. They run through northwestern Wyoming, western Montana, central and northern Idaho, and eastern Washington to the Canadian border. The Northern Rockies include the Bitterroot Range, which Lewis and Clark would cross with great difficulty by means of the Lolo Trail in September 1805. The Northern Rockies also include the Clearwater, Salmon, Sawtooth, and Lost River Mountains and the Front Ranges of Montana.

The Canadian Rockies run north of the Canadian border through British Columbia and Alberta. They include Canada's highest mountain, 12,972-foot Mt. Robson. The fur traders employed by Canada's North West Company found numerous passes through the high peaks of the Canadian Rockies. Particularly significant discoveries included Alexander Mackenzie's crossing of the Rockies in 1793 via the Peace River Pass, and David Thompson's discovery of Howse Pass in 1807 and Athabasca Pass in 1811.

Finally, to the north and west, the Columbia mountain group of the Rockies includes the Selkirk, Purcell, and Cariboo Mountains of Canada and the Brooks Range of Alaska. These remote peaks, extending into the arctic region, were among the last of the Rockies to be explored and climbed; caribou and wolves, rather than humans, remain their principal inhabitants.

When Clark reached the forks in the Jefferson, there was no note from Lewis; a beaver had chewed down the pole on which it had been posted. So Clark, following Lewis's tracks, also headed up the right fork (which was, however, the wrong river). Eventually, everything got straightened out, and on August 7 the reunited party headed up the Beaverhead.

On August 8 they came to another significant landmark, a broad rock formation jutting up from the level valley plain. Lewis recorded the discovery in his journal: "The Indian woman recognized the point of a high plain . . . which she informed us was not very far from the summer retreat of her nation on a river beyond the mountains which runs to the west. This hill she says her nation calls the beaver's head. . . . She assures us that we shall either find her people on this river or on the river immediately west of it's source; which from its present size cannot be very distant."

The next day, August 9, Lewis again headed off overland ahead of the main party, this time with Drouillard, Shields, and McNeal as his companions. They camped that night at a site northeast of present-day Dillon, Montana. On the following day they came to another fork in the Beaverhead. This time, Lewis decided there would be no point in pretending any longer that the water route was still navigable. Here they would have to leave their canoes. Lewis wrote a note to Clark telling him to halt at this spot and wait for his return, attaching it to a dry willow pole (no doubt hoping that this time no industrious beaver would gnaw it down). Meanwhile he was determined to press up the western branch of the divided stream (present-day Horse Prairie Creek), in search of the Shoshone.

On August 11, the explorers set out early as usual. Lewis had the men walk in a spread-out formation, covering a distance of several hundred yards, with Lewis and McNeal in the center together and Drouillard and Shields on the flanks. They had come about five miles in this fashion, searching for signs of Indians, when suddenly Lewis spotted one on horseback, about two miles away across the plain, heading in their direction. Lewis studied the rider through his telescope. The man's clothing was unlike any that Lewis had seen before on an Indian, and so he concluded this must be a Shoshone. "I was overjoyed at the sight of this stranger," Lewis wrote, "and had no doubt of obtaining a friendly introduction to his nation provided I could get near enough to him to convince him of our being whitemen."

When they had closed the distance between them to about a mile, the Indian halted, as did Lewis and McNeal. Lewis took a blanket from his pack and holding it at two corners threw it up into the air and then brought it close to the ground as if spreading it out. He repeated this gesture three times. It was, he had been told by other tribes, a universally recognized sign of peaceful intentions. It may have been, but it did not seem to persuade the distant horsemen of Lewis's goodwill. Meanwhile, Drouillard and Shields, who were spread out to either side of Lewis, continued to walk forward, not having spotted the Indian. Lewis was afraid the two flankers would scare off the rider before he could convince him that they meant no harm. Leaving his rifle with McNeal, he advanced alone. As he did so, he rolled up his sleeve to show off his white skin, holding out trade trinkets in his hand. When he was close enough to be heard by the rider, he called out the word *tab-ba-bone*, which Sacagawea had told him was the Shoshone word for "white man." In reality, the word meant "stranger"—the Shoshone Indians actually had no word for white men since they had never met any.

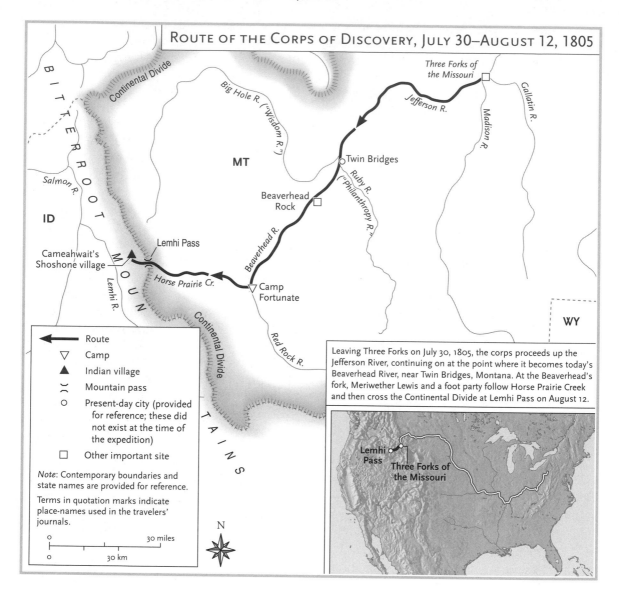

ROUTE OF THE CORPS OF DISCOVERY, JULY 30–AUGUST 12, 1805

Leaving Three Forks on July 30, 1805, the corps proceeds up the Jefferson River, continuing on at the point where it becomes today's Beaverhead River, near Twin Bridges, Montana. At the Beaverhead's fork, Meriwether Lewis and a foot party follow Horse Prairie Creek and then cross the Continental Divide at Lemhi Pass on August 12.

Route

▽ Camp

▲ Indian village

⤙ Mountain pass

○ Present-day city (provided for reference; these did not exist at the time of the expedition)

☐ Other important site

Note: Contemporary boundaries and state names are provided for reference.

Terms in quotation marks indicate place-names used in the travelers' journals.

30 miles

30 km

N

Lewis meanwhile caught Drouillard's attention and signaled him to halt, but Shields missed Lewis's signal and kept heading forward. The rider let Lewis get within about 100 paces, then suddenly turned his horse, whipped him into a gallop and rode off out of sight. There would be no meeting with the Shoshone that day.

Furious at the missed opportunity, Lewis scolded Shields for his "want of attention and imprudence." But at least they now knew that the Shoshone were close by and pressed on eagerly toward the mountains. Lewis fixed a small American flag to a pole; the next time they came in sight of an Indian, he would be ready to display it as a signal of their peaceable intentions (why Lewis thought the Shoshone would recognize or respond favorably to the appearance of the American flag, he did not explain). They came the next day, August 12, 1805, to a "large and plain Indian road" heading up the mountainside. A year and three months into their journey, they stood at the eastern foot of the Continental Divide and were closing in on the headwaters of the great Missouri River. Lewis held hopes of "finding a passage over the mountains and of tasting the waters of the great Columbia" that very evening.

It was not to be so easy.

8

ON FOOT AND ON HORSE ACROSS THE ROCKIES

Captain Lewis and his men did not linger long atop the Continental Divide on August 12, 1805. Although it is easy to imagine Lewis's pride that day, he revealed little in his journal about the moment except his awe at his first view of those "immence ranges" that blocked his view of the western horizon. They still had to find the Shoshone, so this was not the moment to sit around and savor their accomplishment. Soon Lewis and his men headed down the westward slope. After about three-quarters of a mile, they stopped to drink from a "handsome bold running Creek of cold Clear water" which Lewis optimistically described as his first taste of "the water of the Columbia river"—even though he must have already suspected that their arrival at the banks of the real Columbia was still many days away.

They camped that night farther down the slope, by a spring where they made a meager supper from some of the salt pork that they had carried all the way up the Missouri. When they went to sleep, they were spending their first night on foreign territory: Having stepped over the Continental Divide, they had also crossed the bounds of the Louisiana Purchase. They had entered a region that was, as yet, the property of none of the "Great White Fathers" in Washington or London who coveted it. Here, the Indian tribes who inhabited the land remained independent and sovereign. And those Indians were going to be very important to determining the success or failure of the Lewis and Clark expedition in the months to come.

MEETING THE SHOSHONE

The next morning, August 13, they set off early again, heading down into a deep valley. Despite his preoccupation with finding the Shoshone, Lewis typically took the time to examine the new trees and plants they encountered along the route, noting the presence of "white maple" (the Rocky Mountain maple) and "a species of honeysuckle" (the common snowberry). There were more momentous discoveries to come. Walking parallel to the river at the bottom of the valley (the present-day Lemhi River, near Tendoy, Idaho), they spotted a group of Indians about a mile away from them, including a man, two women, and their dogs. The Indians saw them as well. Lewis put down his rifle, unfurled the American flag, and shouted "ta-ba-bone."

But the results were the same as the last encounter. The flag did not reassure the Indians, who took one look at these self-proclaimed "ta-ba-bone," and fled before Lewis could come near enough to prove his good intentions. Only the dogs lingered, and when Lewis tried to tie some trade goods around the neck of one of the animals in a handkerchief, "thinking by this means to persuade [the Shoshone] of our pacific disposition toward them," they too fled.

There was nothing to do but follow the path the Indians had taken. They went about a mile (Lewis noting the presence of prickly pear along the path), when they spied another group of Indians, consisting of "three female savages." There was one elderly woman, one young woman, and a girl of about 12 years of age. The young woman ran off upon spying the whites, while the old woman and the girl remained seated on the ground, heads bowed, apparently resigned to capture or death.

Lewis did everything he could to reassure these two that he meant them no harm. He rolled up his sleeve to show his white skin, (his face and hands, he notes, had by this time been tanned by the sun "quite as dark as their own"). He pressed some trinkets into their hands, and repeated "ta-ba-bone." That seemed to persuade the old woman, and she called to the younger woman who had fled to come back. Lewis dipped his finger in some of the vermillion paint he was carrying as trade goods and painted the "tawny cheeks" of the women, a gesture that was "emblematic of

peace" among the Indians. Using sign language, he convinced them to lead his party to their chief.

They did not have long to wait. Two miles farther down the path, they met up with a band of 60 warriors on horseback who were thundering toward them, apparently summoned by the first group who had fled Lewis and his men. This moment could have spelled disaster for the expedition. The Indians were obviously expecting a hostile raiding party from another tribe and were armed to give battle with their bows and arrows and a few muskets. Coolly and courageously, Lewis advanced toward the riders unarmed, carrying the flag on its pole. One can only imagine the absolute amazement these Shoshone warriors must have felt in seeing this unknown man in a cocked hat come toward them with his piece of red, white, and blue cloth dangling from a stick. The Shoshone women called out to their men that these strangers came bearing gifts and meant no harm. Instantly, the war party became a welcoming party. The chief and other warriors dismounted and rushed to hug Lewis and his men, saying in their own language "I am much pleased, I am much rejoiced." Lewis was, of course, equally happy that the Indians were pleased to meet them, but somewhat less happy that they were so demonstrative of their feelings: "we were all carresed and besmeared with their grease and paint till I was heartily tired of the national hug." But the Corps of Discovery had met the Shoshone at long last.

They sat in a circle on the ground with the chief, whom they discovered was named Cameahwait (a name meaning "The One Who Never Walks"), and smoked some of Lewis's tobacco in a pipe. Lewis handed out more trinkets and gave Cameahwait the American flag he had been carrying when they met,

Salmon served as an essential part of the diet of Indians living along the rivers of the Pacific Northwest, including the Shoshone, Nez Perce, Chinook, and Clatsop tribes. *(U.S. Fish and Wildlife Service)*

"which I informed him was an emblem of peace among whitemen." After smoking a ceremonial pipe, they accompanied Cameahwait and his men about four miles farther down the road, where they came to the tribe's encampment.

Cameahwait's people were the Lemhi Shoshone band, part of the Northern Sho- shone tribe of the Rocky Mountains, also known to Lewis and Clark as the Snake Indi- ans. The Lemhi Shoshone lived a kind of bor- derland existence between two separate Indian ways of life—the river-based, salmon- fishing culture of the Pacific Northwest and the nomadic buffalo hunting culture of the Plains. Part of the year, from May to September, they lived in their preferred setting, the Lemhi River valley west of the Continental Divide and fished; then, reluctantly, they ventured east of the Divide across Lemhi Pass and hunted buffalo on the Plains. It was not a trip they looked forward to, for it held constant danger from raiding parties of Hidatsa, Blackfeet, and other well-armed Indian tribes. As soon as they had enough dried buffalo meat to last through the winter, they returned to the mountains. They were getting ready now to make their annual trek to the plains.

Neither in their own valley nor on the plains had the Shoshone ever encountered white men, though they had a few goods of European manufacture obtained in trade with other tribes. Their poverty, compared to well-established trading tribes such as the Mandan, was evident to Lewis and his men. But the Shoshone were rich in one resource: Cameahwait owned a herd of about 400 horses. As a Virginia gentleman, Lewis knew a thing or two about horse breeding, and he declared in his journal that he would not have been ashamed to ride some of the Shoshone mounts "on the South side of James River" in his home state.

There was more ceremonial smoking of tobacco and exchanges of presents at the riverside encampment. The Shoshone fed the white men from their own meager food supplies, mostly dried cakes made from serviceberries and chokecherries. They had little salmon left from the summer catch, but Lewis was offered a small piece of roasted fish whose taste pleased him immensely for "this was the first salmon I had seen and perfectly convinced me that we were on the waters of the Pacific Ocean."

RETURN TO LEMHI PASS

For all the hugging, smoking, and hospitality displayed by the Shoshone, they had not entirely made up their minds about these white strangers. With Drouillard interpreting by sign language, Lewis explained to Cameahwait that there was "another Chief and a large party of whitemen" coming up the river on the other side of the mountain; that they desired to trade for horses with Cameahwait's people; and that once Lewis returned to the East, he would send many more white men to come with trading goods—including the muskets that the Shoshone desperately needed in order to defend themselves against hostile tribes.

The promise of future trade pleased Cameahwait, and he agreed to return with Lewis to meet up with Clark and the rest of the expedition. But on the morning of August 15, the day they had agreed to head back over the mountains, the Shoshone lost their enthusiasm for the arrangement. Perhaps they suspected some kind of trick: How could they be sure these white strangers were not in league with their enemies the Hidatsa? Eventually Lewis shamed Cameahwait into keeping his word. "I told him if they continued to think thus meanly of us that they might rely on it that no whitemen would ever come to trade with them or bring them arms and ammunition . . . I still hoped that there were some among them who were not affraid to die, that there were men [who] would go with me and convince themselves of the truth of what I had asscerted." Cameahwait would allow no one doubt his bravery; he would go with Lewis, and eventually was able to persuade some of his warriors to accompany him. As they made to leave for Lemhi Pass, the old women of the tribe wept, fearing they would never see their men again. But Lewis, Cameahwait, and the others had not gone far before a whole crowd of villagers, both men and women, decided to join the band and cross the mountains. Lewis was amazed at how quickly and impulsively they changed their minds; the Shoshone, he decided, had a "capricious disposition."

They traveled 40 miles up over the pass and down the forks of the Beaverhead on nearly empty stomachs, for neither white men nor Shoshone had much in the way of provisions left. Drouillard managed to shoot a deer en route, and the famished Shoshone, "poor starved divils," ate its internal organs raw much to Lewis's disgust (although they carefully refrained from touching the rest of the deer meat, which they considered the white men's portion).

The Indians still feared treachery. As they neared the place where Lewis said the other white men awaited them, he and his men were given Shoshone headwear to wear in place of their own hats; if there was an ambush ahead, the white men would not escape being targets. To quiet Shoshone suspicions, Lewis voluntarily gave Cameahwait his gun, and told him in sign language that he could shoot him if they were attacked.

Unfortunately, when they reached the forks of the Beaverhead, neither Clark nor any of his party had yet arrived. Thinking fast, Lewis had Drouillard fetch a note that he left at the campsite for Clark a few days earlier. Showing it to Cameahwait, he told him it was a message from Clark, saying that he would be along the next day with the main party. Cameahwait appeared to accept Lewis's explanation, but some of the Shoshone were suspicious, saying "that we told different stories," as Lewis recorded in his journal. To keep the Shoshone interested, Lewis had told them that there was a woman of their own tribe traveling with the white men up the river. Not only that, Drouillard added, "we had a man with us who was black and had short curling hair." This seemed to astonish the Shoshone, and Lewis concluded that "they seemed quite as anxious to see this monster," meaning York, "as they wer the merchandise which we had to barter for their horses." He slept uneasily that night, fearing that the Shoshone would slip back across the mountain to safety, and in doing so doom the expedition.

A DAY OF REUNIONS

Early the next morning, August 17, Drouillard and several Shoshone set out along the river bank to find Clark. Shortly after 7 A.M., they ran into the expedition as it struggled upstream. Sacagawea was among the first to see Drouillard and his Shoshone companions approach, and according to Clark she "danced for the joyful Sight" because she recognized the Indians as her own people. Soon afterward, Clark's party reached the forks of the Beaverhead, to Lewis's immense relief. Cameahwait greeted the new white chief warmly, bidding him sit on a white buffalo skin and tying small pieces of seashell into Clark's hair in ceremonial greeting. Sacagawea, meanwhile, embraced another young woman who she recognized as a girl who had been captured with her that day five years earlier along the Three Forks, but who unlike Sacagawea had managed to escape her captors.

Then came the most unexpected reunion of all. Lewis and Clark sat down with Cameahwait to smoke a pipe in preparation for negotiations. Sacagawea and Charbonneau were called over to provide translation. As she joined the circle of men, Sacagawea suddenly recognized Cameahwait as her own long-lost brother. Weeping with joy, she ran to Cameahwait, threw her blanket over him, and embraced him. If there had been any question before of Shoshone friendship for these white strangers, it was now a thing of the past. Lewis and Clark would name their meeting place at the forks of the Beaverhead "Camp Fortunate."

Everyone seemed to have a very good time. The Shoshone were impressed by Lewis's air gun, by his dog, Seaman, and by the promised appearance of York—a man, not a monster, as they could now see for themselves. Lewis bought a few horses for some trifles from the expedition's collection of trade goods. Some of the soldiers, Lewis noted in his journal, did some trading of their own and arranged to have "connection" with the "tawney damsels" who had accompanied the Shoshone warriors across Lemhi Pass. Lewis urged his men to make sure they did not anger any Shoshone husbands by paying unwanted attention to their wives, but no problems arose on that score.

August 18 was Lewis's birthday and found him depressed. Perhaps he was feeling let down after the emotional reunions of the previous day. Or perhaps he was just feeling a long way from home, with a long way still to go to reach the Pacific. He had only one close friend on the expedition, William Clark, and Clark was about to set off without him across the Continental Divide to do some advance route-finding.

Whatever the reason for his low spirits, Lewis dwelled at length on his personal shortcomings in his journal: "This day I completed my thirty-first year, and conceived that I had in all human probability now existed about half the period which I am to remain . . . I reflected that I had as yet done but little, very little, indeed, to further the hapiness of the human race or to advance the information of the succeeding generation." He regretted all the time he had wasted in his youth, when he could have been improving himself and learning more. But he resolved, "in future, to live for *mankind,* as I have heretofore lived *for myself.*" Perhaps this res-

olution made Lewis feel better, perhaps not. A little over a week later he stopped making daily journal entries, and with rare exceptions did not resume until January 1 of the following year.

ROUTE-FINDING

That same morning Clark set out with Cameahwait, most of the Shoshone, 11 of his own men, plus Sacagawea and Pomp. Cameahwait had already warned Lewis of the difficulties the rivers west of the Continental Divide presented to travelers, but the white men took axes with them to build canoes if Clark should find a water route that looked promising. Lewis would remain behind for the moment with the rest of the Corps of Discovery. They prepared a cache for supplies and sank the dugouts with stones in a nearby pond, preserving them for future use. Lewis set his men to work manufacturing wooden packsaddles for carrying supplies, waiting for Cameahwait's promised return with the horses they needed if they were going to get their supplies over the mountains.

When the advance party reached the Shoshone encampment on the Lemhi River, Clark questioned Cameahwait about the path that lay ahead of the expedition. Until this time they had followed directions given the previous winter by the Hidatsa; but the Hidatsa knew little, except by hearsay, of the land to the west of the Rockies. Lewis and Clark had expected to find the "southern fork" of the Columbia when they crossed the Continental Divide. But, as they now were coming to understand, there was no southern fork of the Columbia. Could they travel by tributary streams to the Columbia? If so, they could still preserve the essence of President Jefferson's dream of finding a mostly water-borne passageway across the continent.

The Lemhi River intersected another larger river (the present-day Salmon) a few miles to the north. The Salmon headed north and then its main fork headed westward, the direction they wanted to go. That sounded promising, but Cameahwait told Clark that the fast-running Salmon, which cut through a deep canyon with impassable slopes, would not suit their purpose.

There was another route, Cameahwait told Clark, although it involved a long overland trek. They could follow the banks of the Salmon River's north fork, then push on over a rough trail through steep hills into another river valley (the present-day Bitterroot Valley). Eventually they would find a westward trail that led to a pass through even higher mountains than they had already encountered. They would find little to eat in the high country in this season. But there were Indians who regularly used the trail to travel back and forth to buffalo country. These were the "persed [pierced] nosed Indians" who lived on a river that "ran a great way toward the seting sun and finally lost itself in a great lake of water which was illy taisted and where the white men lived."

The description of the ill-tasting great lake sounded to Clark like the Pacific, their ultimate destination. And if Indians could take the trail across the western mountains, white men could as well. For Clark, Cameahwait's words "instantly settled" for him the question of which way the expedition should go. Cautious as always, he still intended to explore the Salmon River route just to make sure Cameahwait was not exaggerating its difficulties. He and his men set out upriver with a Shoshone guide named Old Toby, but they did not get far. Cameahwait had not exaggerated the difficulty of the river route. They would have to go by land over the mountains after all. The hard-to-kill notion of a short-portage water route to

the Pacific finally died with Clark's brief exploration of the Salmon River.

Having seen Clark off on his foray up the Salmon, Cameahwait headed back across Lemhi Pass to join Lewis at Camp Fortunate, accompanied by Sacagawea, Charbonneau, and about 50 Shoshone. They did more horse-trading. Lewis bought nine horses and a mule from the Shoshone and rented two others, and then with supplies loaded on the newly made packsaddles, he headed back over the pass on August 24. Cameahwait wanted to please his new white friends, who had been good to his sister, and who promised to bring trade—and guns—to the Shoshone. But there was a problem. They were heading west, away from the buffalo. The whites wanted the Shoshone to stay camped along the Lemhi River while they purchased still more horses from them. Cameahwait's people were famished and needed to come east to the buffalo plains as soon as possible. So, while promising Lewis to accompany him all the way back to the Shoshone encampment, he secretly sent some of his men out on the morning of August 25 to alert the rest of his band that it was time to break camp and move east.

Sacagawea now gave a very clear indication that her loyalties lay with the Americans, and not with her own tribe. Having learned of Cameahwait's secret plan, she told Charbonneau. Her husband, who did not seem to think it was very important news, finally got around to mentioning Cameahwait's plan to Lewis several hours later. "I was out of patience with the folly of Charbono," Lewis fumed in a journal entry. The Frenchman "had not sufficient sagacity to see the consequences which would inevitably flow from such a movement of the indians . . ." If the Shoshone headed east in the next day or so, then they could not trade with them for more horses, which would be a disaster for the expedition.

Lewis confronted Cameahwait. He once again threatened and shamed the Shoshone chief. If Cameahwait failed to honor his promise to the expedition, Lewis would guarantee that no whites would ever come and trade arms to the Shoshone. The chief "remained silent for some time, [but] at length he told me that he knew he had done wrong but that he had been induced to that measure from seeing all his people hungary. . . ." Cameahwait agreed to send another messenger ahead to tell his people to remain in their encampment. The expedition was saved, though Lewis did not seem to fully appreciate the sacrifice that the Shoshone were making on behalf of the self-righteous white strangers.

Lewis and his men reached the Shoshone encampment on August 26. That night there was fiddle music and dancing, "much to the amusement and gratification of the natives." Cameahwait had promised that there would be horse-trading on the next day, but Lewis spent another uneasy night fearing "that the caprice of the indians might suddenly induce them to withhold their horses from us . . ."

Lewis got his horses, although not the sleek mounts he had admired in their herd. The Shoshone were becoming shrewder traders and made the white men pay a high price in their trade goods for a collection of old and ailing nags, not at all the kind of animals that Lewis would have chosen to ride back home in Virginia. There was nothing to be done about it. They needed mounts, and now they had them, 29 horses and one mule. Clark rejoined Lewis at the Shoshone encampment on August 29, and on the following day, guided by Old Toby and his son, they said goodbye to Cameahwait and set out overland up the Lemhi River and then up the north fork of the Salmon River. The ankle-deep snow through which they slogged over the rough terrain reminded them again of the need to push on as hard and fast as they could before the onset of winter.

FLATHEAD COUNTRY

The Corps of Discovery left the banks of the Salmon River behind and crossed over what later became known as Lost Trail Pass on September 3, dropping down the following day into easier traveling country in the Bitterroot Valley. Here, they met another tribe of Indians, the Flathead or Salish tribe, who were camped at a site near present-day Ross's Hole, Montana. "[T]hose people recved us friendly," Clark wrote in his journal, "threw white robes [over] our Sholders & Smoked in the pipes of peace."

The "Flathead" name was misleading. Some Indian tribes in the Northwest bound the heads of infants with boards to shape their growing skulls with a slanted or "flattened" forehead, which they considered a mark of beauty. The Salish did not follow this practice, but since they lived in the region where Lewis and Clark expected to find head-flattening, they called them by that name anyway. Lewis and Clark also marveled to hear the Salish speak a language that, to their ears, sounded remarkably like Welsh; the myth of the Welsh Indians died even harder than the myth of the short portage across the Rockies.

They bought more horses from the Salish, who also generously exchanged some of their fresh mounts for the broken-down Shoshone cast-offs in the expedition's herd. With their 40 or so horses they could lighten the packs each animal carried, so they made good time as they headed north alongside the Bitterroot River. Lining the broad river valley on both sides were mountain ranges— to the east the relatively gentle Sapphire Mountains, but to the west, the direction they would have to cross, the higher, more jagged,

Contrary to the name Lewis and Clark knew them by, Flathead Indians did not, in fact, flatten their heads. This painting, done by James W. Alden in 1857, shows a camp and the clearing of land along the Flathead River. *(National Archives [NWDNC-76-E221-ALDEN45])*

and increasingly snow-covered Bitterroot Mountains. Under other circumstances the scenery might have inspired them, but their stomachs were empty and they did not care. On September 6 Clark noted bleakly that there was "nothing to eate but berries, our flour out, and but little Corn, the hunters killed 2 pheasents only . . ." Several days of hard rain did nothing to lift their spirits.

THE HARDEST STRETCH

On September 9 the Corps of Discovery camped on a "fine bould clear running stream," which entered the Bitterroot River from the west, about 10 miles south of present-day Missoula, Montana. They called this stream Traveler's Rest Creek (it was later known as Lolo Creek). Old Toby gave them news there that was both discouraging and encouraging. To the east lay a trail alongside a river (present-day Big Blackfoot River). If they followed that trail over the mountains to the east, they would come to an easy pass, and in just four days they would reach the Missouri River near the Great Falls. The previous winter the Hidatsa had tried to tell them about this pass, but they had misunderstood the directions they had been given. As a result, they had wasted nearly two months traveling south to the headwaters of the Missouri before heading up a parallel path northward along the Salmon and Bitterroot Rivers. (Of course, if they had crossed at the earlier opportunity, they would have done so without the benefit of horses.) The encouraging aspect of Old Toby's news was that, on their return trip, they could make much better time heading for home if they followed his suggested route.

Meanwhile, there were high mountains to the west still to be crossed. The men did not look forward to what lay ahead. "The snow makes them look like the middle of winter,"

Joseph Whitehouse wrote in his journal of the Bitterroots; they were "the most terrible mountains that I ever beheld," according to Sergeant Gass.

On September 11 the Corps of Discovery set out along what has come to be called the Lolo Trail. For 11 cold, hungry, weary days they struggled across the Bitterroots. Horses slipped on the steep footing and rolled down the hillsides, scattering the expedition's supplies. That no one was killed or injured en route seems a miracle. But the phrase *much fatigued* appeared day after day in Clark's

journal. Bad weather added to their woes. What was rain in the Bitterroot Valley turned to snow in the Bitterroot Range. Eight inches of snow fell on September 16, and Clark wrote in his journal that "I have been as wet and as cold in every part as I ever was in my life."

Everything else might have been endurable, had it not been for hunger. The place names they bestowed en route serve to commemorate their days of travel on meager rations: There was "Killed Colt Creek" where they stopped to eat one of the colts in their herd, and "Hungery Creek" where they failed

This photograph taken by Edward Curtis in about 1910 shows four Salish (Flathead) women sitting on the ground preparing meat, probably in much the same way as they had at the time of Lewis and Clark. *(Library of Congress, Prints and Photographs Division [LOT 12327-A])*

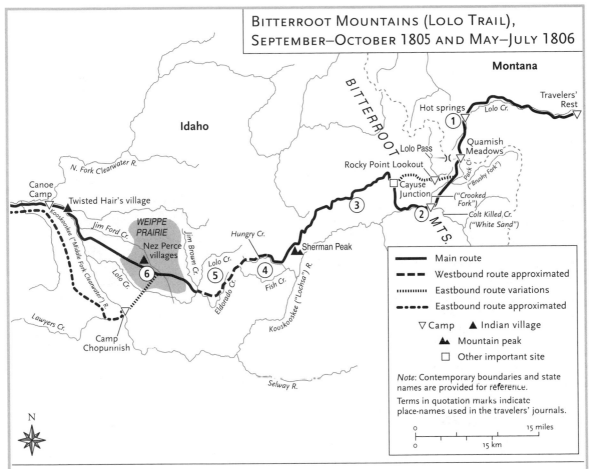

BITTERROOT MOUNTAINS (LOLO TRAIL), SEPTEMBER–OCTOBER 1805 AND MAY–JULY 1806

1. "When we had gone 2 miles, we came to a most beautiful warm spring, the water of which is considerably above the blood-heat; and I could not bear my hand in it without unpleasantness."
   —Patrick Gass, September 13, 1805

2. ". . . encamped opposit a Small Island at the mouth of a branch on the right side of the river. . . . Here we were compelled to kill a colt for our men & selves to eat for the want of meat & we named the south fork Colt Killed Creek, . . ."
   —William Clark, September 14, 1805

3. "Some of the men without Socks, wrapped rags on their feet, and loaded up our horses and Set out without any-thing to eat and proceeded on. Could hardly See the old trail for the Snow."
   —Joseph Whitehouse, September 16, 1805

4. "Encamped on a bold running creek passing to the left which I call *Hungery* Creek as at that place we had nothing to eate."
   —William Clark, September 18, 1805

5. "The men are becoming lean and debilitated, on account of the scarcity and poor quality of the provisions on which we subsist . . . We have, however, some hopes of getting soon out of this horrible mountainous desert . . ."
   —Patrick Gass, September 19, 1805

6. "At 12 miles descended the mountain to a leavel pine country. Proceeded on . . . to a small plain in which I found main Indian lodges. Those people gave us a small piece of buffalow meat, some dried salmon beries & roots. . . . They call themselves *Cho pun-nish* or *Pierced noses*."
   —William Clark, September 20, 1805

Note: Original spelling and punctuation have been retained from journal entries.

The Corps of Discovery trekked across the Bitterroot Mountains to the Clearwater River by way of the Lolo Trail, a historic Indian hunting and trade route. *(Montana Historical Society, Helena)*

to have even that poor a meal. Normally, four deer were required to feed the expedition; in their 11 days in the Bitterroots, they managed to kill only five deer, little more than a single day's ration. The howling coyotes did not make for restful nights, but Captain Lewis killed one and it went into the pot to feed the men, as did a few grouse, one duck, and some crayfish. They were eventually reduced to eating some of the "portable" (dried) soup they had lugged all the way up the Missouri; it must have been a truly vile concoction, because if there was anything else to eat—even coyote—they avoided it. They also consumed 20 pounds of the candles they carried.

NEZ PERCE HOSPITALITY

On September 18, with the expedition still floundering over the snowy hills of the Bitterroots, Clark set off ahead of the main party with six men in search of open country and better hunting. Two days later, on September 20, Clark and his party reached the Weippe Prairie in present-day Clearwater County,

Idaho, 160 miles from their starting point at Traveler's Rest. There they came across an encampment of Nez Perce Indians. They were directed by the Indians to another encampment on the Clearwater River, where they met a Nez Perce chief named Twisted Hair.

Like the Shoshone, most of the Nez Perce had never encountered white men. According to Nez Perce tradition, the tribe debated what to do about the strangers. Some thought they should kill them and take their rifles and other goods. An old woman named Watkuweis, who like Sacagawea had been captured by a rival Indian tribe, was the only Nez Perce who had ever seen whites before. Fortunately her experience with whites (probably French traders) had been good. "These are the people who helped me," she said of the whites. "Do them no hurt."

The Nez Perce fed the famished white strangers on dried salmon and a bread made from camas roots. (The camas plant, a form of lily common in the West, produced a blue flower in the spring; when it lost its flowers, the Nez Perce and other Indian tribes would dig up the bulbs, steam, and then dry them, and grind them into flour.) Clark and his men ate heartily, but unfortunately they found that the new diet did not sit well in their famished stomachs. "I find myself verry unwell all the evening," Clark wrote in his journal on September 20, "from eating the fish & roots too freely." The next day was no better: "I am very sick today," Clark wrote on the 21, "and puke which relive me." Clark treated himself and his men with Rush's Pills, a powerful laxative that only increased their stomach miseries. When Lewis and the rest of the party stumbled

Lewis and Clark's diplomatic efforts are illustrated in the above etching by Patrick Gass of the two men holding council with Indians. *(Library of Congress, Prints and Photographs Division [LC-USZ62-17372])*

down out of the Bitterroot Range on September 22, Clark tried to warn them to go easy on the salmon and camas roots, but to no avail. They stuffed themselves, as starving people will, and soon were as sick as Clark and his men. (It is likely that their illness was due to bacteria in the fish.)

Despite their illness, Lewis and Clark carried out their duties as diplomats, handing out Jefferson medals to Twisted Hair and several other chiefs. Twisted Hair drew them a map on a piece of white elk skin showing how to travel by lesser rivers westward to the river which flowed directly to the sea. He and another chief named Tetoharsky also agreed to accompany Lewis and Clark through Nez Perce territory as far as the Columbia.

On September 26 Clark, accompanied by Twisted Hair and several other Nez Perce Indians, established the "Canoe Camp" on a site five miles west of present-day Orofino, Idaho. The new camp was on the south bank of what Lewis and Clark would call in Nez Perce language the Kooskooskee River

The Nez Perce Horses

Meriwether Lewis greatly admired the horses possessed by the Indian tribes west of the Rockies. In February 1806 he would write in his journal: "Their horses appear to be of an excellent race; they are lofty eligantly formed active and durable; in short many of them look like fine English coarsers and would make a figure in any country."

Spanish explorers introduced horses to the North American continent in the mid-16th century. No other European import had as dramatic an impact on the lives of western Indians as the horse. When the Indians acquired horses, they swiftly changed long-established patterns of settlement, warfare, hunting, and trading. The introduction of the horse allowed tribes living in the river valleys west of the Rockies to venture eastward across the mountains to hunt buffalo, while at the same time increasing the risk of conflict with the Plains-dwelling Indians such as the Lakota.

The Nez Perce had first acquired horses around 1700. They used their horses for transportation on their yearly migration west of the Rockies, when whole villages would migrate from the valleys of the Columbia, Snake, and Clearwater Rivers to higher elevations where they would gather camas roots and fruit, hunt, and fish the mountain streams.

The Nez Perce became known as expert horse breeders. Appaloosa horses, with their distinctive spotted coats, were often to be found in Nez Perce herds. Lewis described the Appaloosa breed in his journal as "pided [pied] with large spots of white irregularly scattered and intermixed with the black brown bey [reddish brown] or some other dark color. . . ." (The term *Appaloosa* is derived from the Palouse River, which flows through eastern Washington.) The Nez Perce valued their horses highly. They painted their coats and decorated their halters and saddles with beads, dye, and porcupine quills.

(the present-day middle fork of the Clearwater River). Virtually all the Corps of Discovery were still recovering from stomach ailments (Lewis suffering intensely, and Clark feeling only a little better). But with the help of the Nez Perce they soon built five dugout canoes, this time out of ponderosa pines rather than the cottonwoods they had relied on along the Missouri. The Indians showed them how to burn out the interior of felled trees to save labor. By October 6 their new fleet was complete. They branded the 38 horses that had survived the trip over Lolo Trail and turned them over to the care of the Nez Perce, burying their saddles and some other supplies.

Finally on the afternoon of October 7, the Corps of Discovery proceeded on down the Clearwater River in their new dugout canoes. The short portage they had expected to find connecting the waters of the Missouri to the waters of the Columbia had turned into an arduous land journey of two months' duration and some 400 miles of rugged terrain. It must have been a great relief to the footsore soldiers to find themselves once again riding in canoes, instead of bushwhacking through rough and broken country. Even better, they were traveling with the current, instead of against it as they had all the long way up the Missouri River. The Clearwater River was flowing toward the Pacific.

9

"OCIAN IN VIEW!"
To the Pacific

Lewis was still feeling sick to his stomach when the expedition resumed its journey on water, this time setting off in its little fleet on the waters of the Clearwater River. Clark recorded the last-minute confusion that attended the Corps of Discovery's departure on October 7: "[A]s we were about to set off we missd. both of the Chiefs who promised to accompany us; I also missed my Pipe Tomahawk which Could not be found." The pipe tomahawk never turned up that day, but the chiefs did the following day, October 8, when Twisted Hair and Tetoharsky boarded the expedition's dugouts near a village a few miles west of Canoe Camp. There was more confusion on October 9, when Old Toby and his son suddenly departed without collecting the pay they were owed for five weeks' service guiding the expedition, including the terrible week and a half the Corps of Discovery had spent crossing the Bitterroot Mountains. The captains never knew what scared off their heretofore intrepid Shoshone guides, though it may have been the sight of the fast-flowing Clearwater River or the prospect of traveling among strange Indians in territory so far from home. Lewis and Clark asked the Nez Perce chiefs to send a horseman to bring back Old Toby and his son so they could be properly compensated but were told it would be pointless; anything the white men gave the Shoshone guide would be taken from him by the Nez Perce Indians whose villages he would have to pass before reaching the protection of his own tribe.

DOWN THE CLEARWATER

The dangers of the Clearwater were not to be underestimated. On the expedition's first day on the river, one of the canoes struck a rock and sprung a leak. Fortunately it remained afloat, and the men were able to repair it that night. Notwithstanding the mishap, the Corps of Discovery made 20 miles on the Clearwater that day. After making a further 18 miles the next day, another canoe, piloted by Sergeant Gass, struck a rock. Filling rapidly with water with water through a leak in its side, it over-

On October 8, 1805, the rapids of the Grand River sent one of the corps' canoes crashing into a broken tree-top. This etching made by Sergeant Patrick Gass shows the canoe sinking, but none of the crew members' journal entries of the day seem stark. Rather, the men were eager to describe the Indian tribe they met soon after. *(Library of Congress, Prints and Photographs Division [LC-USZ62-19232])*

turned, dumping men and supplies in the rapids. The expedition laid up on a nearby island on October 9 to dry their goods and make further repairs.

Stuck on the shore, the explorers found themselves the object of great curiosity on the part of the local Indian population. They usually welcomed such attention, but this time the curiosity they attracted was not entirely innocent. "The Indians troublesom," Clark noted on the 9: "Stole my Spoon." Theft had not been a problem until now. When they traveled up the Missouri and crossed the Rockies, the Corps of Discovery had been able to welcome Indians into their midst without the least thought for protecting their belongings; as Lewis wrote of the Shoshone, notwith-

standing their "extreem poverty" they were "extreemly honest."

The tribes they encountered along the Clearwater, Snake, and Columbia Rivers displayed a different attitude toward expedition property. They apparently did not think the whites would notice or care much if a few small and useful items disappeared from their packs and canoes. If the Corps of Discovery had still been as well equipped as it was when setting off up the Missouri, that might have proven the case. But at this stage of their journey, every spoon counted.

DOWN THE SNAKE

On October 10 the explorers set off again down the Clearwater and, despite yet another near-disastrous encounter between a canoe and a rock, managed to cover an extraordinary 60 miles of river that day, the farthest they had ever come in a single day. That night they slept at the confluence of the Clearwater and the Snake Rivers. (Their journey that day also took them across the border from present-day Idaho to present-day Washington.)

As the corps headed westward, the country along the river changed dramatically. They left the mountains and high meadows behind and found themselves in a region of rolling hills and canyons. The ponderosa pines that they had passed along the shores of the Clearwater disappeared: There was now "no timber of any kind," Clark noted in his journal on October 12 as they sailed down the Snake. They had passed through vast tracts of treeless land before. But in the Great Plains they found cottonwood trees to camp among along the river bottom. The waving grasses of the prairie lands, at least along the Lower Missouri, suggested to them the possibility of raising crops and building settlements. They could imagine white settlers following in their wake. Along the Snake, Clark complained, nothing grew by the riverside but "a fiew Hack berry bushes and willows. . . ." In the even drier terrain to come when they reached the eastern Columbia, sagebrush would dominate the landscape. Lewis, who was once again leaving the daily journal-keeping to Clark, was not moved to any of the rapturous descriptions of the countryside to compare with his appreciation for the Lower Missouri, the mouth of the Yellowstone, or the Missouri Breaks.

Compared to their struggle getting across the Bitterroots the month before, they were making good progress. But river travel, even with the advantage of a favorable current, was still strenuous. Although they had hired three Indian guides to help them navigate the Snake's rapids, they could not avoid frequent spills, costing them irreplaceable supplies and valuable time. A dugout piloted by Drouillard struck a rock on October 14 and sank, along with blankets, tomahawks, shot pouches, and other goods. In five days on the Snake, they traveled less than 120 miles.

ON TO THE COLUMBIA

On October 16 they reached the junction of the Snake and the Columbia Rivers, 3,714 miles from their starting point on the Mississippi River. Clark was very matter-of-fact in his description of the day's events: "[H]aving taken our Diner Set Out and proceeded on Seven miles to the junction of this river [the Snake] and the Columbia which joins from the N.W." Clark's understated response should not obscure the significance of the moment, for the Corps of Discovery's arrival at the Columbia rivaled the crossing of the Continental Divide in its importance in the history of the Lewis and Clark expedition. It had been 13 years since an American merchant captain, Robert Gray, had discovered the river's mouth on the Pacific. If Jefferson's dream of a water route across the continent was no longer viable, his soldiers had nonetheless found a route linking the major river crossing the Plains with the major river that flowed to the Pacific.

The Corps of Discovery came upon the Columbia more than halfway along the river's 1,210-mile course to the sea. The headwaters of the river, which Lewis and Clark never saw, were to be found in a lake deep in Canadian territory, in present-day British Columbia. For its first 200 miles the river flows northwestward, before bending to the south. A hundred miles below the present-day U.S.-Canadian border, the river bends westward and continues more or less due west to the Pacific. It is the second-longest river in the Americas emptying in the Pacific (Canada's and Alaska's Yukon River is the longest.) When they reached the confluence of the Snake and the Columbia, Lewis and Clark were back on a river that had already been explored by white men, from its mouth on the Pacific to a distance of about 100 miles inland. They were thus linked again to the world they had known in the East, as well as on the last stretch of their journey to the western edge of the conti-

nent. But they still had some 400 miles of treacherous waters to navigate ahead of them.

As they traveled along the river, Lewis and Clark found new reasons to be glad they had brought Sacagawea along with them. Clark noted in his journal on October 13: "The wife of Shabono our interpetr we find reconsiles all the Indians, as to our friendly intentions—a woman with a party of men is a token of peace." The two Nez Perce chiefs, Twisted Hair and Tetoharsky, accompanying the expedition

This photograph taken by Edward Curtis in December 1910, is of Chinook Indians sitting in a canoe by the shore of the Columbia River. Reaching the river, the gateway to the Pacific, was one of the expedition's most momentous successes. *(Library of Congress, Prints and Photographs Division [LC-USZ62-47010])*

The Columbia River Salmon Culture

The lands they were passing through may have seemed barren and inhospitable to the Corps of Discovery, but the waters cutting through them in the deep river valleys of the region were richly endowed with migratory salmon. The Indians who lived along the river fed themselves from its bounty. While no single Indian community along the Columbia was as large or permanently established as the Mandan villages, the region was as thickly populated as any Lewis and Clark would pass through on their journey. Every few miles the expedition came across another small riverside settlement of timber-framed lodgings with rush mats covering walls and roofs, and as Clark noted, "large Scaffols of fish drying at every lodge . . ." The salmon was as important to the peoples who lived along the rivers of the Pacific Northwest as the buffalo was to the peoples who lived along the upper Missouri River.

Salmon endured a strenuous life cycle. Born in freshwater, newly hatched salmon made their way hundreds of miles down streams and rivers to the ocean, where they grew into adults. Every year, between mid-April and mid-October, vast numbers of adult salmon (perhaps as many as 16 million) would swim back from the ocean through the freshwaters of the Columbia and its tributary rivers, branching off from the rivers to the exact stream where they had been born. There they would spawn their eggs, renewing the life cycle, and dying soon afterward. The Indians along the rivers would harvest the fish as they made their annual runs upstream. Lewis and Clark recorded the existence of a number of varieties of salmon they encountered on the Columbia and its tributaries: the silver or coho salmon, the king or chinook salmon, the blue-backed or sockeye salmon, as well as the related species, the steelhead trout.

on this stretch of its journey also served as a sign that the white men were not to be feared or attacked. They set off ahead of the expedition, announcing its coming to the Indian bands in fishing encampments along the river. The tribes in this region were related to the Nez Perce, and spoke dialects of the same language, known to later generations of linguists as Sahaptian.

Twisted Hair and Tetoharsky's advance work helped win a particularly friendly reception for the Corps of Discovery when they came upon the junction of the Snake and Columbia. The arrival of the white explorers

provided a welcome distraction to the Yakama and Wanapam Indians who were camped there, drying fish and repairing their gear at the end of the annual salmon run. Clark recorded that the local chief came to see them "at the head of about 200 men Singing and beeting on their drums . . ." The Indians formed a half circle around the white men "and Sung for Some time . . ."

They spent two days camped at the confluence of the Snake and Columbia. Back among Indians who were "of a mild disposition and friendly disposed," the captains took advantage of the opportunity to practice some diplomacy. They smoked a peace pipe with the chief, and they put on the same show they had perfected a year earlier, heading up the Missouri. They handed out Jefferson medals and made a speech informing the gathering "of our friendly disposition to all nations, and our joy in Seeing those of our Children around us." The Yakama and Wanapam were technically nobody's "children" at that moment, because neither the Great White Father in Washington or his rival in London had yet established valid claim to the lands along the Columbia or the Snake. But Lewis and Clark's words made clear that they thought it was only a matter of time before the land on the western side of the Continental Divide, like that to the east, would become part of the United States. For their part, the local Indians were not troubled by the question of where the actual territorial boundaries of the United States ended in 1805; it could not have seemed like a question that would ever have much effect on their lives.

From the Wanapam chief Cutssahnem, and from another Yakama chief whose name went unrecorded, the explorers received maps of the Columbia that included information on what Indian tribes might be expected along their route. On October 18 they set sail down the last of the rivers they would follow to the Pacific. Sergeant Gass recorded in his journal entry for the day that "we proceeded down the Great Columbia, which is a very beautiful river."

On their first day on the Columbia, they encountered the Walla Walla tribe near the mouth of a river that bore their name. The chief, named Yellepit, "a bold handsom Indian, with a dignified countenance about 35 years of age . . .," according to Clark, gave them another friendly reception. Yellepit brought the whites a basket of berries as a gift, and in turn he received one of the Jefferson medals. The chief wanted Lewis and Clark to stay and visit with his tribe for a while. But, keenly conscious of the approach of winter, the captains begged off, promising to stay longer with the Walla Walla on their return trip.

DIFFICULT WATERS

The Corps of Discovery at first enjoyed smooth sailing on the broad waters of the Columbia. Measuring the river on October 18, Clark found it stretched nearly 1,000 yards from one bank to the other. But they soon discovered that the Columbia would not be an easy highway to the ocean. On October 22 the expedition's canoes came to what Lewis and Clark called the Great Falls of the Columbia, later known as Celilo Falls, where the river's elevation dropped 38 1/2 feet in a complicated series of falls and cataracts. The excellent fishing opportunities offered by the narrowing of the river at Celilo Falls had attracted Indians to the area for the past 10,000 years, making it one of the longest-settled communities in North America. To Lewis and Clark, however, it was just an obstacle. To get safely past the worst of these falls, they portaged their supplies along a narrow trail on the northern shore of the Columbia, near present-day Wishram, Washington, then crossed the river and hauled their dugouts along the southern shore.

One challenge was quickly followed by the next on this stretch of the river. On October 24 the river narrowed dramatically at a point near the present-day city of The Dalles, Oregon. All the water that had moved placidly down the Columbia where it was 1,000 yards wide was now pinched into a channel, which at its narrowest stretched a mere 45 yards from bank to bank. Clark described this passage of the river as an "agitated gut swelling, boiling & whorling in every direction." The corps had to get through two sets of daunting rapids, called the Short Narrows and the Long Narrows. They considered another portage, but decided it would take too much time. Instead, with their most experienced boatsmen at the helm, they ran the canoes down the narrows. Much to the astonishment of the Indians who were watching from the riverbanks and clearly expected the foolish white men to drown in the attempt, they passed the narrows without mishap.

The river was changing, and so were the peoples who lived along it. The riverbank along the Short and Long Narrows, like the Mandan villages, functioned as a center of trade that drew Indians up and down the river from many tribes. It also served as a linguistic and cultural dividing line. To the west of the Narrows, peace prevailed among the tribes speaking Sahaptian languages, stretching all the way to the Rockies; to the east of the Narrows, peace prevailed among the tribes who spoke languages of the Chinookan family, stretching all the way to the Pacific. But relations between the Sahaptian- and Chinookan-speaking tribes were not peaceful. Twisted

The overhead view of Celilo Falls in this photograph aptly represents the vastness of the falls and why Lewis and Clark named the landmark the Great Falls of the Columbia. *(Library of Congress, Prints and Photographs Division [LC-USZ62-107043])*

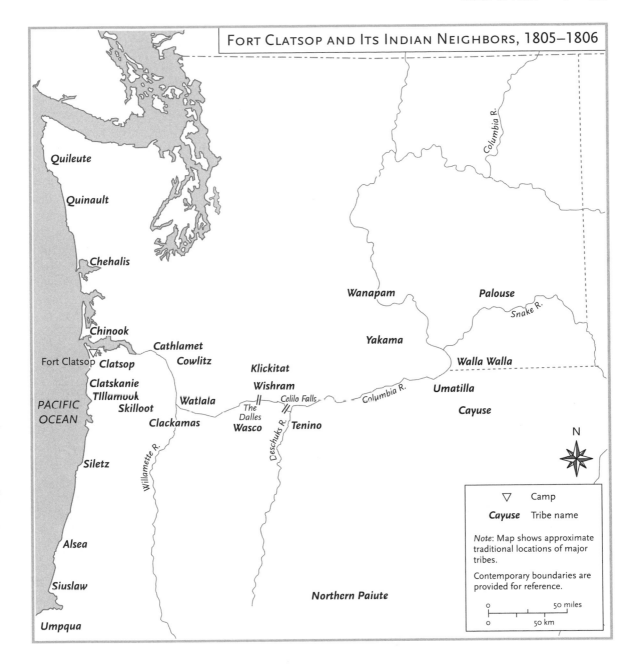

FORT CLATSOP AND ITS INDIAN NEIGHBORS, 1805–1806

Quileute

Quinault

Chehalis

Chinook

Fort Clatsop Clatsop

Clatskanie
Tillamook
Skilloot

PACIFIC
OCEAN

Cathlamet
Cowlitz

Watlala

Clackamas

Siletz

Alsea

Siuslaw

Umpqua

Klickitat

Wishram
Celilo Falls
The
Dalles
Wasco

Tenino

Wanapam

Yakama

Walla Walla

Umatilla

Cayuse

Palouse

Snake R.

Columbia R.

Willamette R.

Deschutes R.

Columbia R.

Northern Paiute

N

▽ Camp

Cayuse Tribe name

Note: Map shows approximate
traditional locations of major
tribes.

Contemporary boundaries are
provided for reference.

0   50 miles

0   50 km

Hair and Tetoharsky knew that if they went any further they would be straying into hostile territory, and for several days they had been saying they wanted to turn back and go home. Lewis and Clark persuaded them to stay with the expedition at least until they passed the Narrows, to give them a chance to broker peace between the tribes. The Nez Perce chiefs agreed but warned the captains to be on their guard against attack by the Chinookan tribes.

Lewis and Clark held their council on the evening of October 24, after their successful descent of the Narrows. A chief from the Wishram-Wasco band of Chinookan-speaking people came to their camp along with some of his warriors, providing "a favorable opportunity of bringing about a Piece," Clark thought. They smoked pipes, handed out medals, and urged the tribes of the lower and upper Columbia to put aside their weapons. "[W]e have every reason to believe," Clark wrote confidently in his journal that night, "that those two bands of nations are and will be on the most friendly terms with each other." But the captains were again indulging in the wishful thinking that so often characterized their ventures into Indian diplomacy. Twisted Hair and Tetoharsky headed home the next day, anxious to return to the safety of Sahaptian-speaking territory. The Corps of Discovery was once again on its own.

THE WESTERN COLUMBIA

Not far past the Narrows, the corps confronted yet another pinched-in portion of the river, this one known as the Upper and Lower Cascades. This stretch seemed even more daunting than the Narrows, and the captains decided to portage their goods and dugouts rather than push their luck any further. Below the cascades, on October 31 they found a "remarkable high detached rock" on the north shore of the Columbia, a volcanic plug almost 900 feet in height, which they named Beacon Rock.

Although they were still more than 100 miles from the ocean, they began to feel the effects of the tides on the river; before they had traveled much farther, the river water would prove so salty they had to rely on rainwater to drink. Of that there would prove to be no shortage. The mountains they were now passing on either side of the river worked a dramatic change in the climate.

On their very first day on the Columbia, back on October 18, Clark noted that they had seen "a mountain bearing S.W. Conocal form Covered with Snow." On the next day, a second mountain came into view, "a high mountain of emence hight covered with Snow." The first mountain he left nameless for the moment; the second, Clark decided, "must be one of the mountains laid down by Vancouver, as Seen from the mouth of the Columbia River"—that is, one of the mountains that the British naval officer William Broughton under the command of Captain George Vancouver had discovered and named in 1792. "I take it to be Mt. St. Helens," Clark wrote—though it was, in fact, Mount Adams, for Mount St. Helens is still hidden from view on that portion of the river. Looking back on November 3 in the direction from which they had come, Clark again saw the tall snow-capped peak that he had spotted on October 18 and left unnamed. He now realized that it must be Mount Hood, a high glacier-covered volcanic cone also named by Lieutenant Broughton. They soon reached the mouth of a river entering the southern side of the Columbia, a tributary they called the Quicksand (the present-day Sandy River). This was the highest point on the Columbia River reached by Broughton in his reconnaissance of 1792. Thus, for the first time since April, they were back in territory previously visited by whites.

Mount Hood, Mount St. Helens, and Mount Adams were all part of the Cascade Range, a volcanic ridge averaging 5,000 feet in height, dotted with glaciated peaks that reached twice that height or more. The Cascades ran up the western edge of the continent, roughly 100 miles from the coast, from northern California through the present-day states of Oregon and Washington. The Columbia River provided one of the few open paths through this mountainous barrier, in a region later known as the Columbia Gorge. As they passed through the Cascades, the Corps of Discovery left behind the open hills and semi-desert conditions of the eastern end of the gorge and entered a region of deep forests and lush undergrowth. East of the Cascades,

annual rainfall is limited to about six inches; west of the Cascades, 10 times as much falls every year, as the rain clouds perpetually rolling in from the Pacific bump up against the mountains and go no further.

The explorers were in a hurry to get to the ocean, and they never stayed more than a night with any of the Chinook Indians whose wooden plank houses they passed along the river. White men, or at least the goods that white men had to offer, were no novelty to

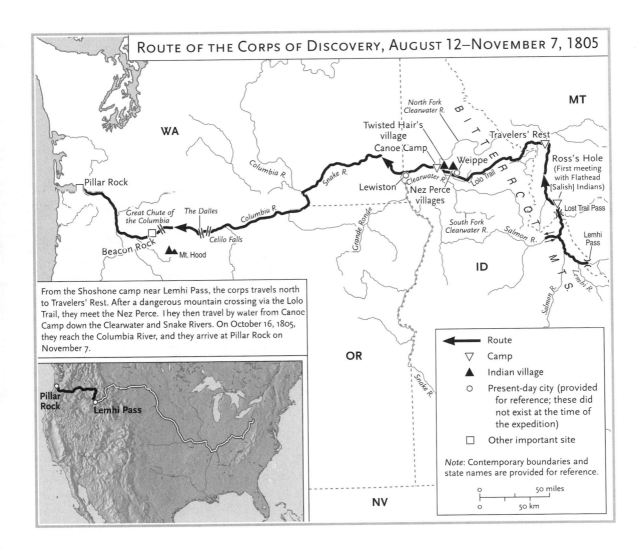

ROUTE OF THE CORPS OF DISCOVERY, AUGUST 12–NOVEMBER 7, 1805

From the Shoshone camp near Lemhi Pass, the corps travels north to Travelers' Rest. After a dangerous mountain crossing via the Lolo Trail, they meet the Nez Perce. They then travel by water from Canoe Camp down the Clearwater and Snake Rivers. On October 16, 1805, they reach the Columbia River, and they arrive at Pillar Rock on November 7.

these Indians. The corps saw one Indian wearing a sailor's jacket, others wearing scarlet and blue blankets. There were iron pots, brass teakettles, and muskets in the villages. They even began hearing a few words of spoken English, suggesting both the proximity of white traders and the rough nature of their conversations (among the recognizable words Lewis recorded hearing from Indians they now encountered was "musquit, powder, shot, knife, file, damned rascal, sun of a bitch, etc."). Another less-than-welcome sign of frequent contact with white merchants was the fact that the Chinook knew the value of the things they offered to sell the expedition, especially food. "They asc high prices for what they Sell," Clark complained on November 1, "and Say that the white people below give great prices for every thing. . . ."

Their dislike of the local Indians mounted as they found themselves besieged by light-fingered visitors. Clark had a pipe tomahawk stolen on November 4 in a tense encounter with a band of Skilloot Indians on an island on the southern shore of the Columbia they called Wappatoe Island (present-day Sauvie Island); a few days later, three Indians were caught in the act of stealing a knife; a few days after that, Shannon and Willard's guns were stolen, though recovered when the white men confronted the thieves. Clark warned one group of visiting Indians that if they tried to steal guns or other expedition goods, "the men would Certainly shute them . . ."

AT LAST THE PACIFIC

All their troubles were momentarily forgotten on November 7, as they sailed down a stretch of the river near present-day Altoona, Washington. They knew the Pacific could not be far off. That afternoon, as they proceeded on down the Columbia in their canoes, they could see the river widen dramatically and could hear the sound of waves crashing on the shore ahead. Without any attempt to dis-

This photograph captures the sun setting over the Columbia Gorge in Oregon. *(Library of Congress, Prints and Photographs Division [LC-USF3427-004795-A])*

guise his emotions, Clark set down in the pages of his field journal the most famous sentence he would ever write: "<u>Ocian in view!</u> O! the joy."

It would make a better story if Clark were right; unfortunately, he was mistaken. The waves were genuine enough, but they were crashing in Gray's Bay, part of the Columbia estuary, not the edge of the Pacific at all. They still had 20 miles of the Columbia to proceed down before they would reach the ocean. And those would not be an easy 20 miles.

The Pacific Northwest winter was settling in, and it was the worst time to be navigating the Columbia estuary in clumsy dugout canoes. Driving rain and high waves cut short their river travel on November 8; "the Canoes roled in Such a manner as to cause Several [expedition members] to be verry Sick," Clark reported. For two miserable days they camped on a tiny beachhead on the northern side of Gray's Bay. A lull in the storm on November 10 let them gain an additional eight miles down the river, to Point Ellice, near present-day Meglar, Washington. There they were trapped again by bad weather for several more days. Everything was wet; no one could sleep; they were cold and exhausted. "A hard rain all the last night . . ." Clark wrote on November 11; "a tremendious thunder Storm abt. 3 oClock this morning. . . .", he wrote on November 12; "The rain Continue all day," he wrote on November 13. It did not help anybody's spirits that there was "nothing to eate but pounded fish which we Keep as a reserve and use in Situations of this kind."

Finally, on the afternoon of November 15, after 11 days of more or less continuous downpour ("the most disagreeable time I have experienced" according to Clark), the rain briefly relented and they were able to sail down to Chinook Point, still on the Columbia estuary but in sight of the ocean. There they camped for the next nine days, finding shelter in huts built from lumber they took from an abandoned Indian village. Meanwhile Lewis and a small group hiked to the end of Cape Disappointment, where Lewis carved his initials in a tree and then walked along the ocean beach. It was Clark's turn to visit the ocean with another party a few days later. The "men

appear much Satisfied with their trip beholding with estonishment the high waves dashing against the rocks & this emence ocian" he wrote on November 18. On November 19 Clark's party walked about nine miles up the coast, to about the site of present-day Long Beach, Washington, where he carved his name and the date on a small pine tree.

At the end of their journey to the Pacific, they could take stock of the immensity of their accomplishment. Back at Camp Wood in the winter of 1803–04, Clark had made estimates of the distance they would have to travel to reach their final destination. His estimates had proven reasonably accurate as long as they traveled through the previously explored Lower Missouri. But his estimate of the distance from the Mandan village to the Pacific—1,550 miles—was off by 1,000 miles. They had traveled roughly 2,550 miles between April and November 1805. All told, by the new estimate Clark recorded on November 16, 1805, they had come 4,142 miles from the mouth of the Missouri to the mouth of the Columbia.

Now that they had seen the ocean, some members of the Corps of Discovery were in favor of heading back up the Columbia for a drier climate. "[M]en all Chearfull," Clark wrote on November 18, "express a desire to winter near the falls [Celilo Falls] this winter." Lewis and Clark disagreed. Disagreeable as the ocean climate was, the temperatures were relatively mild, and they feared it would be much colder inland. The shoreline north of the Columbia offered little game, but they had been told by the Clatsop Indians who lived on the southern shore that elk were abundant in the woods there. If they moved their camp to the south, they could feed themselves on elk meat during the winter and use the elk skins to manufacture new clothing and moccasins. They could also make salt from the ocean water to preserve and flavor their food. Not only that, but if they stayed by the ocean for the winter, they might encounter an American or British merchant ship, which would enable them to purchase supplies for themselves, and trade goods to carry back with them on their return journey. They might even be able to send a copy of their journals back with the ship, thus increasing the chances that the record of their expedition would reach Jefferson should any evil end befall them on the return.

Again, as when they faced a critical choice at Decision Point at the mouth of the Marias River, the captains could have simply issued an order. Instead Lewis and Clark put the question to a vote on November 24, and after some debate the proposal to cross the Columbia and seek a winter encampment site near the ocean got the most votes (the other votes were divided between "falls" and "SR"—the Sandy River). All of the men were allowed to participate in the vote, including Clark's slave, York. Sacagawea's preference was noted as well, though not counted in Clark's final tally of the voting; she was listed as being "in favour of a place where there is plenty of Potas [potatoes, or roots]."

FORT CLATSOP

They crossed to the south bank of the Columbia on November 26 and remained camped there for the next week and a half. Lewis took a party inland, and he found a spot for a winter encampment in the forest near a freshwater spring, three miles up a small river that is now known as the Lewis and Clark River (and is about five miles southeast of present-day Astoria, Oregon). They moved to the site on December 7 and started building their third and final winter encampment, called Fort Clatsop after the local Indian tribe.

The new fort was square, enclosing an area about 50 feet square, with two long barracks rows facing each other across a small parade ground, and gates in both the front and back walls. The captains had a room to themselves in the barracks, as did Charbonneau and his family. The enlisted men bunked eight to a room. The fort was not designed for comfort, but at least it provided a roof over their heads. They needed one. Of the 161 days they would spend at Fort Clatsop, they would enjoy only 12 days without rain.

The third Christmas of the expedition afforded only a meager celebration. "Our Diner to day," Clark wrote in a morose entry on December 25, "Consisted of pore Elk boiled, Spilt [spoiled] fish & Some roots, a bad Christmass diner . . ." On January 1, 1806, the captains were awakened by a volley fired by

A large member of the deer family, the elk is related to the moose. When the expedition spent the winter on the Oregon coast, elk was a staple of their diet and eventually the members lost their appetite for it. *(National Park Service)*

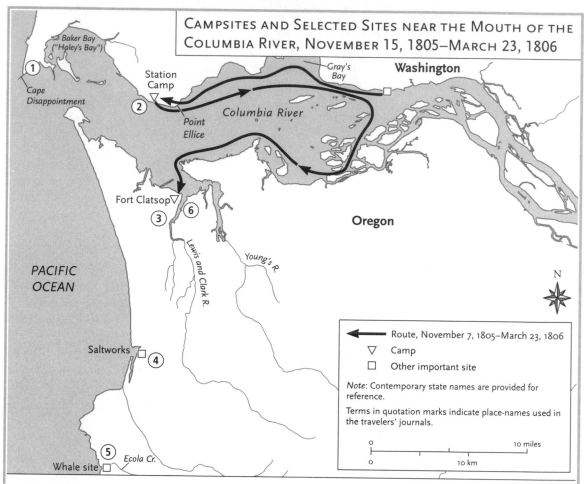

CAMPSITES AND SELECTED SITES NEAR THE MOUTH OF THE COLUMBIA RIVER, NOVEMBER 15, 1805–MARCH 23, 1806

Baker Bay ("Haley's Bay")

Cape Disappointment

Station Camp

Gray's Bay

Washington

Point Ellice

Columbia River

Fort Clatsop

Oregon

Lewis and Clark R.

Young's R.

PACIFIC OCEAN

Saltworks

N

Route, November 7, 1805–March 23, 1806
▽ Camp
□ Other important site

Note: Contemporary state names are provided for reference.

Terms in quotation marks indicate place-names used in the travelers' journals.

0   10 miles
0   10 km

Whale site

Ecola Cr.

1. "Here I found Capt. Lewis name on a tree. I also engraved my name, & by land the day of the month and year, as also several of the men."
    —William Clark, November 18, 1805

2. "In the Evening our Officers had the whole party assembled in order to consult which place would be the best, for us to take up our Winter Quarters at. The greater part of our Men were of opinion; that it would be best, to cross the River, . . . "
    —Joseph Whitehouse, November 24, 1805

3. "at day light this morning we we[re] awoke by the discharge of the fire arms of all our party & a Selute, Shoute and a Song which the whole party joined in under our windows, after which they retired to their rooms were Chearfull all the morning."
    —William Clark, December 25, 1805

4. "About noon Captain Clarke with 14 men came to the saltmakers camp, in their way to the place where the large fish had been driven on shore, some distance beyond this camp."
    —Patrick Gass, January 7, 1806

5. "I . . . thank providence for directing the whale to us; and think him much more kind to us than he was to jonah, having Sent this monster to be Swallowed by us in Sted of Swallowing of us as jonah's did.
    —William Clark, January 8, 1806

6. "the rain Seased and it became fair. about meridian at which time we loaded our canoes & at 1 P.M. left Fort Clatsop on our homeward bound journey. at this place we had wintered and remained from the 7th of Decr 1805 to this day, and have lived as well as we had any right to expect, . . . "
    —John Ordway, March 23, 1806

Note: Original spelling and punctuation have been retained from journal entries.

the men outside their cabin to mark the arrival of the New Year. A year before they had celebrated the New Year with their Mandan friends. Now they were looking forward to spending the next New Year back in their own homes, where, as Lewis wrote (in his first journal entry in many months), "we hope to participate in the mirth and hilarity of the day."

After Christmas and the New Year, there were few diversions to break up the monotony. One came on January 5, when they received a report from local Indians of a whale washed up on the beach a few miles south of the fort (at present-day Cannon Beach, Oregon). Hoping to obtain something to eat other than elk and salmon, and eager for an outing, Clark prepared to set out to find the whale. Much to the captains' surprise, Sacagawea virtually demanded to be included in Clark's party. "The Indian woman was very impo[r]tunate to be permitted to go," Lewis wrote in his journal, "and was therefore indulged; she observed that she had traveled a long way with us to see the great waters, and that now that monstrous fish was also to be seen, she thought it very hard she could not be permitted to see either (she had never yet been to the Ocean)."

Sacagawea got her wish and saw the ocean; of the "monstrous fish," there was not much left by the time they got to it on January 8; Indians from the local Tillamook tribe had gotten there first and stripped off all the meat and blubber. But the trip was not wasted; apart from the chance to get away from the confines of the fort for a little while, they also purchased 300 pounds of blubber and some whale oil from the Indians. The whale proved a welcome if exotic addition to their diet and was entirely consumed by the end of January. We "prize it highly," Lewis wrote and, thinking of the Old Testament story of how the prophet Jonah was swallowed by a whale, praised God for "having sent this monster to be *swallowed by us* in stead of *swallowing of us* as jona's did."

THOUGHTS OF HOME

Whenever they were in sight of the ocean, they kept an eye peeled for the sails of a merchant ship. But none appeared. There would be no news from home and no opportunity to send copies of their journals to Jefferson by sea. Most critically, they would be unable to replenish their dwindling supply of trade goods (now only about enough to fill two handkerchiefs, according to Lewis.) It was going to be a frugal trip back to St. Louis.

They made do with what they had at hand. There was game to be hunted and meat to be preserved. They turned elk skins into clothing and moccasins to replace the worn and rotting garments and footwear they had worn down the Columbia. In late December some of the men set up a camp on the seacoast (in present-day Seaside, Oregon) to make salt. They boiled saltwater in five large kettles, scraping out the salt left when all the water had boiled off; over the next two months they produced four bushels of salt. Lewis pronounced the salt to be "excellent, fine, strong & white" and reported with gusto how much more he was enjoying his food now that it could be seasoned.

As he had the previous winter at Fort Mandan, Clark now devoted his time to mapmaking, noting in his journal on February 14: "I have compleated a _map_ of the Counterey through which we have been passing from the Mississippi at the Mouth of the Missouri to this place." The Corps of Discovery, he claimed optimistically, had succeeded in finding "the most practicable and navigable passage across the Continent of North America."

of small fish which now begin to run an, are
taken in great quantities in the Columbia R.
about 40 miles above us by means of skiming
or scooping nets. on this page I have drawn
the likeness of them as large as life; it
as perfect as I can make it with my
pen and will serve to give a
general idea of the fish. the
rays of the fins are boney but
not sharp tho' somewhat pointed.
the small fin on the back
next to the tail has no
rays of bone being a
bonanous pellicle.
to the gills have
each. those of the
eight each, those
are 20 and 2.
that of the back
the fins are of
is of a bleuish
the the lower
is of a silve-
nart. the
behind the
second of
the purple
a silver
and
like

thin men
the fins next
eleven rays
abdomen have
of the pinneani
half formed in front.
has eleven rays. all
a white colour. the back
duskey colour and that of
part of the sides and belley
onf white. no spots on any
first bone of the gills next
eye is of a bleuis cast, and the
a light goald colour nearly white
of the eye is black and the iris of
white. the under jaw exceeds the uper,
the mouth opens to great extent, folding
that of the herring. it has no teeth.
the abdomen is obtuse and smooth, in this
differing from the herring, shad anchovey
&c of the Malacapterygious Order & Class
Clupea

This detailed drawing of a eulachon (commonly referred to as a candlefish) was
made by Lewis in his journal. Surrounding the illustration are Lewis's thorough
notes on his observations of the fish. (American Philosophical Society)

While Clark drew his maps, Lewis wrote long, descriptive entries in his journals cataloging the plant and animal life of the Oregon country, as well as recording observations of Chinookan customs, dress, and appearance. Lewis also displayed his talents as an artist; the pages of his journal from that winter are filled with images that came to symbolize the discoveries of the Corps of Discovery, including his drawing of a eulachon or candlefish, an oily fish related to the smelt that ran up the Columbia in large numbers in late spring and proved another welcome bit of variety at mealtime. "I find them best when cooked in the Indian stile, which is by roasting a number of them together on a wooden spit . . ." Lewis wrote with obvious zest. "They are so fat they require no additional sauce, and I think them superior to any fish I ever tasted"—certainly to "pounded salmon," which he was consuming altogether too often.

The captains knew there was no point in heading east too soon. Although the Columbia, unlike the Missouri, never froze over, an early spring start would only bring them to a dead halt once they reached the snowbound Rockies. They were not going to be able to get across that formidable barrier any time before June, at the earliest. But life at Fort Clatsop, an unending round of rain-soaked days, flea-bitten nights, and spoiled elk meat at meal-time, proved too much to bear. They had originally planned to set off eastward on the Columbia on April 1, but by early March they had decided to leave as soon as possible.

But there was another problem. They no longer had enough canoes to carry all of their party. Only three of their dugouts remained seaworthy. Lewis traded his uniform coat for an Indian canoe, but they could not find another one available for a price they were willing to pay. And so, notwithstanding their own complaints about "thievish Indians," they decided to steal another canoe from the local Clatsop Indians, who had been very friendly to them throughout the winter. The theft of the Clatsop canoe was not the Corps of Discovery's finest moment.

By mid-March, their preparations were made except for the final packing of the canoes, but then, typically, the weather turned bad. They waited impatiently through another four days of steady rain. On March 22, Lewis vowed that the expedition would leave the next day "at all events." As it turned out, the weather finally cooperated, with the rain stopping about midday on March 23. Wasting no time, the men hurriedly packed their belongings and themselves into their three dugouts and two Indian canoes, and at 1 P.M. they proceeded on up the Columbia. The Corps of Discovery was going home.

10

HOMEWARD BOUND

Another long winter came to an end for the Corps of Discovery. It had now been more than 22 months since they had first "proceeded on" up the Missouri. The men paddling their rough dugouts and canoes against the current were long-haired, bearded, and probably none too clean, dressed from head to foot in elk skin. In appearance, apart from their Harpers Ferry rifles and a few other stray bits of military gear, little would have suggested that this was a detachment of the U.S. Army.

Whatever they lacked in spit and polish, they made up for in energy. These men were happy to be heading home. They paddled 16 miles upriver on March 23, their first day back on the Columbia, and another 16 the next day; a few days later they would make 20 miles. That was an excellent rate of speed, considering they were now fighting the current that flowed down to the Pacific, and considering that the river was swollen with the spring melt-off of mountain snows. Within a week they had arrived back at Wappatoe Island (present-day Sauvie Island). The weather was still disagreeably cold when they woke in the mornings, but signs of

spring were all around, including the blackberries and dogwoods coming into bloom along the river.

On the expedition's second day on the river, an Indian paddled out to reclaim the canoe they had stolen a week earlier. They paid him off with an elk skin. That was not much of a trade from the Indian's perspective. Lewis insisted in his journal that the man "consented very willingly" to the exchange, but then a lone Indian was not in a good position to haggle with 30 heavily armed men, who were not intending to return the canoe in any case.

A NEW RIVER AND A NEW MOUNTAIN

Heading up the river, the men could see Mount Hood and Mount St. Helens again, their slopes wearing a full mantle of wintry white. Lewis took a more careful and approving look at the surrounding landscape than he had managed coming downriver; he now judged the stretch of the Columbia west of the Cascades "the only desireable situation for a

This photograph of a canoe is a more modern version of the ones used by Lewis and Clark. In the distance is Wind Mountain, which is in the Columbia River Gorge area. *(Library of Congress, Prints and Photographs Division [LC-USZ62-47012])*

settlement which I have seen on the West side of the Rocky mountains."

By the end of March, they were camped along the north side of the Columbia near the site of present-day Washougal, Washington. Their early departure from Fort Clatsop was now working to their disadvantage. On their first week on the river they had bought dried fish from Indians they encountered en route, including sturgeon and eulachon. But the fish that those who lived along the Columbia depended upon above all others, the salmon, had yet to make its annual appearance. Without a supply of fresh salmon, the local Indians were going to have a hard time feeding themselves, let alone 33 strangers passing upriver.

Lewis and Clark decided they would have to halt for a week and restock their larder with venison and elk meat. There was another advantage to stopping where they did. Local Indians told them of a southern tributary of the Columbia whose mouth, hidden by Wappatoe Island, lay a few miles to the west. The delay provided the opportunity for a side trip to explore this river, known to the Indians as the Multnomah, and later to be renamed the Willamette.

On April 3 Clark led seven men back down the Columbia to the mouth of the Willamette River and then a further 12 miles up the Willamette to the site of the present-day city of Portland, Oregon. They spotted a new snow-covered "noble mountain" to the south, another of the Cascade peaks, which they named Mount Jefferson. Lewis and Clark imagined the Willamette to be a much greater river than it actually proved to be, thinking wishfully that it would provide a river highway all the way down to southern California. In fact, its headwaters were to be found a scant 200 miles away in the southern Cascade Mountains.

Clark and his men rejoined the main body of the expedition the following day, and on April 6 the Corps of Discovery resumed their trip up the Columbia. Lewis noted they passed "several beautifull cascades which fell from a great hight," including one falling nearly 300 feet (probably present-day Multnomah Falls). By mid-April they had reached the stretch of narrows, rapids, and falls east of the Cascades, which they surmounted by portaging their supplies on land while pulling the empty canoes and dugouts upstream with towropes from the shore.

BAD MOOD ON THE COLUMBIA

As on their trip down the river, they were again harassed by Indians intent on helping themselves to expedition property. On April 11, during the portage below The Dalles, local Indians enraged Lewis when they made off with Seaman. Lewis sent out a party of three men to retrieve the dog, telling them to shoot the thieves if necessary (they got the dog back without violence). Shortly afterward another Indian attempted to make off with an ax, which was also recovered. Lewis posted a sentinel to keep all Indians out of the camp "an informed them by signs that if they made any further attempts to steal our property or insulted our men we should put them to instant death." When an Indian stole a small piece of iron on April 21, Lewis struck the man, which, as Sergeant Gass noted, "was the first act of the kind, that had happened during the expedition."

The captains were eager to stop fighting the river currents and strike off overland instead. For that they would need horses, and the local Indians were not eager to sell them any, at least not at prices they could afford from their meager remaining supply of trade

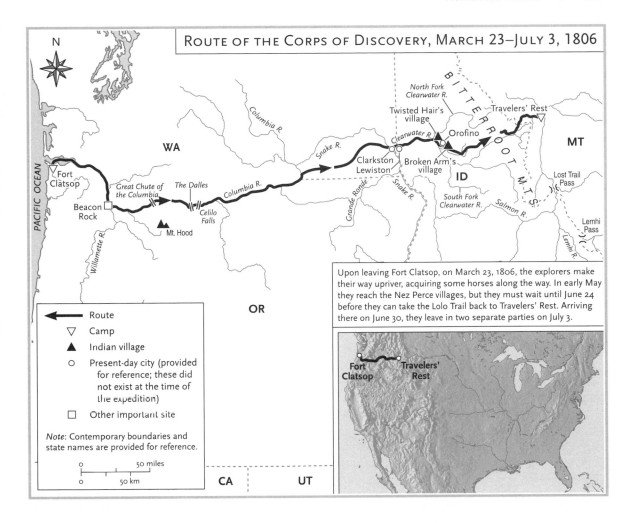

ROUTE OF THE CORPS OF DISCOVERY, MARCH 23–JULY 3, 1806

Upon leaving Fort Clatsop, on March 23, 1806, the explorers make their way upriver, acquiring some horses along the way. In early May they reach the Nez Perce villages, but they must wait until June 24 before they can take the Lolo Trail back to Travelers' Rest. Arriving there on June 30, they leave in two separate parties on July 3.

Route
▽ Camp
▲ Indian village
○ Present-day city (provided for reference; these did not exist at the time of the expedition)
□ Other important site

Note: Contemporary boundaries and state names are provided for reference.

50 miles
50 km

goods. Clark spent several days in mid-April negotiating with Indians on the north side of the Columbia, and he was able to purchase only a few broken-down mounts. "These people are very fathless [faithless] in Contracts," Clark complained in his journal on April 19; time and again Clark thought he had sealed an agreement for the purchase of a horse, only to have the seller come back a few hours later and demand additional payments, or cancel the sale entirely. Lewis and the rest of the party crossed the Columbia several days later

to join Clark. By trading off their cooking kettles they acquired a few more horses—10 in all, not nearly enough. Rather than abandon their dugout canoes to the local Indians, they chopped the vessels up for firewood.

On April 21 the expedition set off on land along the north shore of the Columbia. A few of the men were assigned to paddle upriver in the two Indian canoes, which carried gear that could not fit on their horses. The expedition eventually traded the remaining two canoes for some beads to increase their trade goods, and they managed to pick up a few more horses in trading with Indians they met along the way.

On April 27 they met up again with the Walla Walla chief Yellepit, who had been so welcoming on their trip down the Columbia the previous fall. Yellepit was "much gratifyed" to see them return, and they spent several days with him at his tribe's encampment near the mouth of the Walla Walla river. The Indians brought them firewood and some fish (the salmon were now running again), and the expedition was able to add additional horses to their herd. Lewis and Clark were relieved to be back among friendly and cooperative Indians who "behaved themselves in every risepct extreemly well," as Lewis noted. Yellepit presented Clark with a "very eligant white horse," and Clark presented the chief with a sword and some gunpowder and musket balls. Yellepit also told them of a "good road" with plenty of game that would cut eighty miles

The Umatilla lived near the Walla Walla in present-day Oregon. Three Umatilla Indians are shown standing by their camp on the shore of the Columbia River in this photograph taken by Ralph Irving Griffin ca. 1922. Tipis were not traditionally used by this tribe; at the time of Lewis and Clark's visit, they lived in plank houses. *(Library of Congress, Prints and Photographs Division [LC-USZ62-115455])*

from their return journey, heading inland over territory that was new to them until reconnecting with the Snake just south of its confluence with the Clearwater. With Yellepit's help they crossed the Columbia and left that river behind them for good.

BACK AMONG THE NEZ PERCE

They reached the Snake River on May 4. Although they were now back among the Nez Perce, a tribe they had gotten along with well the previous year, Lewis was still finding it hard to live up to Jefferson's instructions to treat the Indians they encountered "in the most friendly & conciliatory manner," as he showed at the midday meal on May 5. Lewis wrote in his journal that evening:

> while at dinner an Indian fellow verry impertinently threw a poor half starved puppy nearly into my plait by way of derision for our eating dogs and laughed very heartily . . . I was so provoked at his insolence that I caught the puppy and threw it with great violence at him and struk him in the breast and the face, siezed my tomahawk and shewed him by signs if he repeated his insolence I would tommahawk him, the fellow withdrew apparently much mortifyed and I continued my repast *on dog* without further molestation.

A few days later they met up again with their old friend Chief Twisted Hair at a site near present-day Orofino, Idaho. The Nez Perce had kept their horses for them over the winter and returned the 21 they were able to round up to the explorers. Lewis and Clark's men dug up the saddles and ammunition they had left in a cache by the Clearwater River.

At a council with Nez Perce chiefs, Lewis returned to his role as diplomat, urging the tribe to seek peace with other tribes in the region. At the same time, and somewhat inconsistently, he described the great advantages that would soon come to the Nez Perce through trade with the Americans, notably guns to defend themselves against their enemies the Blackfeet. He also urged the Nez Perce to send a representative east to meet Thomas Jefferson—although the president was not yet the Great White Father of the Nez Perce, because the tribe lived in a territory west of the Rockies. The Nez Perce were uninterested in making such a long journey eastward in any case, but they did agree to send some young men with Lewis and Clark across the Bitterroot Mountains to talk peace with the Shoshone.

Just when they would be able to make that crossing of the mountains was a source of considerable concern to the captains. The Indians told Lewis and Clark that they could not think of attempting the mountains anytime soon due to the winter snows that had yet to melt; it would be another month before the Bitterroots were passable. "This is unwelcom inteligence to men confined to a diet of horsebeef and roots," Lewis noted in his journal, "and who are as anxious as we are to return to the fat plains of the Missouri and thence to our native homes." On May 14 they moved their camp a few miles eastward, to a site on the north bank of the Clearwater River near present-day Kamiah, Idaho. They would remain at this encampment from May 13 through June 9. It would prove the longest the Corps of Discovery would remain at any one place along the entire route, except for their winter encampments at Fort Mandan and Fort Clatsop. Later generations of historians labeled this site Camp Chopunnish. ("Chopunnish" was a name the explorers used for the Nez Perce.)

While they waited, they did what they could to increase their provisions for crossing the Bitterroots: "[N]ot any of us," Lewis wrote, "have yet forgotten our sufferings in those mountains . . ." The captains divided up the remaining stock of trade goods among the men and ordered them to trade with the Nez Perce for edible roots to add to their stock of rations. Lewis and Clark even cut the brass buttons from their coats to trade for more roots.

Despite their impatience to resume their journey eastward, the Corps of Discovery were happy to spend more time among the Nez Perce. Lewis called the tribe "the most hospitable, honest and sincere people that we have met with in our voyage." In turn, the Nez Perce seemed to genuinely like the explorers, especially Clark who was much valued as a healer. Dozens of Indians visited him at Camp Chopunnish to be treated for everything from sore eyes to paralysis. Clark did what he could for them, with his small supply of pills and limited medical knowledge, and seems to have cured some of his patients and relieved others of the worst of their symptoms. Relations between the Nez Perce and the whites were also made stronger with dances, footraces, target shooting contests, and other games. According to stories later told by the Nez Perce, William Clark fathered a son by a Nez Perce woman that spring, although there is no clear proof of his paternity. Lewis meanwhile kept up his study of western animals and plants, describing in his journals birds new to science such as the western tanager and a root crop called *cous* that the Nez Perce used to make bread.

BACK ACROSS THE BITTERROOTS

May turned to June, and the Nez Perce were still warning the captains that it was too soon to attempt the Bitterroots. But the captains decided to press ahead, and the men approved: as Lewis noted on June 9, "our party seem much elated with the idea of moving on towards their friends and country." The following day the Corps of Discovery loaded their horses (they now had a fine herd of 70) and set out to the east. They stopped at Weippe Prairie, where they had first met the Nez Perce the previous fall, and spent several days there hunting and preserving meat. On June 15 they headed up into the mountains.

They soon realized they should have listened to the Nez Perce. The horses floundered in the deep snow and could find no grass to eat. The expedition made it as far as Hungry Creek, a place of unhappy memory, but the captains decided on June 17 that they would have to turn back. It was "the first time since we have been on this long tour," Lewis noted, "that we have ever been compelled to retreat . . ." Some of the men "were a good deel dejected."

The captains sent Drouillard and Shannon to ride back ahead of the main party to the Nez Perce camp, asking for guides to join them at Weippe Meadow for their next attempt on the Bitterroots. On June 23 their couriers returned with three "young men of good character" from the Nez Perce. Two others had already joined their party planning to go east to meet with Flathead (Salish) Indians. On June 24 they set out again over the Bitterroots with their Nez Perce companions, and this time successfully crossed the mountains. Having expert guides made a big difference. Much of the snow had melted in the interval, revealing patches of grass for the horses. On June 30 they arrived at Traveler's Rest. It had taken them 11 days to cross the mountains heading west in fall 1805; in spring 1806 they completed the return trip in just six days.

DIVIDING THEIR FORCES

During the winter at Fort Clatsop the captains had pored over their trail maps and made a daring decision. There were so many tantalizing blank spaces to fill in on Clark's maps that they would need to split up when they reached Traveler's Rest. It was a complicated plan that depended a good deal on luck and timing to pull off. Lewis would lead a detachment eastward across the mountain pass that their Shoshone guide Old Toby had told them about the previous fall, a shortcut back to the Great Falls of the Missouri. At the Great Falls, Lewis would divide his party again, taking half of them on an overland route back to the Marias River. Lewis planned to follow the Marias northward to see how far it traveled towards the rich fur country of the Saskatchewan region.

Meanwhile, Clark was to lead the other half of the party back down the Bitterroot valley, through which they had traveled in the fall. They would not retrace their route exactly, however, but would cross the Rockies by a new mountain pass, which would bring them back to Camp Fortunate and from there to the Three Forks of the Missouri by a shorter route than the one they had followed across Lemhi Pass in summer 1805. At Three Forks Clark would divide his own party. Half his men would take the canoes they had cached at Camp Fortunate down the Missouri to rendezvous with the men who Lewis left at the Great Falls. Clark would proceed on overland to the Yellowstone River, and follow it back to

In this etching by Patrick Gass, Captain Lewis is shown in the only fight that took place on the entire expedition. When the Blackfeet did not respond to his threat, Lewis raised his gun and shot one of them.
(Library of Congress, Prints and Photographs Division [LC-USZ62-19231])

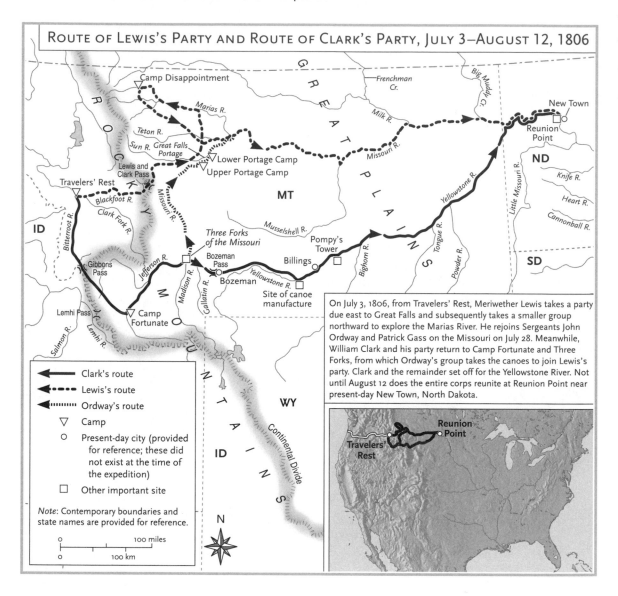

ROUTE OF LEWIS'S PARTY AND ROUTE OF CLARK'S PARTY, JULY 3–AUGUST 12, 1806

On July 3, 1806, from Travelers' Rest, Meriwether Lewis takes a party due east to Great Falls and subsequently takes a smaller group northward to explore the Marias River. He rejoins Sergeants John Ordway and Patrick Gass on the Missouri on July 28. Meanwhile, William Clark and his party return to Camp Fortunate and Three Forks, from which Ordway's group takes the canoes to join Lewis's party. Clark and the remainder set off for the Yellowstone River. Not until August 12 does the entire corps reunite at Reunion Point near present-day New Town, North Dakota.

Clark's route
Lewis's route
Ordway's route
▽ Camp
○ Present-day city (provided for reference; these did not exist at the time of the expedition)
□ Other important site

Note: Contemporary boundaries and state names are provided for reference.

its mouth on the Missouri. The men at Great Falls would continue down the Missouri, rendezvousing with Lewis en route, and proceeding on until they, too, came to the mouth of the Yellowstone, where Lewis and Clark and the entire Corps of Discovery would reunite.

Lewis and Clark said good-bye to each other on the morning of July 3, after a few days at Traveler's Rest, recovering from the crossing of the Bitterroots. "I took leave of my worthy friend and companion, Capt. Clark, and the party that accompanyed him," Lewis wrote in his journal that evening. "I could not avoid feeling much concern on this occasion although I hoped this seperation was only momentary."

Lewis and nine of them men rode north along the Bitterroot River, accompanied by the five Nez Perce, and then turned east along Clark's Fork river. The Nez Perce left them on July 4, but said they could not miss the trail through the mountains, and as proved usual when the Nez Perce gave directions, they knew what they were talking about. The pass over which Lewis and his men crossed the Continental Divide is now known as Lewis and Clark Pass. On July 11 they reached the site of their former camp at White Bears Island on the Missouri. The trip overland from Traveler's Rest had taken them just eight days. They also killed a buffalo on July 11, their first taste of their favorite meat since the previous summer. Less happily, unseen Indian thieves made off with 10 of their 17 horses that night.

Meanwhile, Clark's party followed a separate route back to the Missouri. They, too, made rapid progress, traveling south on horseback down the Bitterroot valley. On July 4, 1806, they celebrated their third Independence Day on the trail. This time there was no whiskey to salute the occasion, but they did stop early in the day for a "Sumptious Dinner" of venison. On July 6 they crossed the Continental Divide by way of a mountain pass now known as Gibbons Pass. On July 8 they reached the site of Camp Fortunate on the Beaverhead River, the place where Sacagawea had enjoyed her reunion with her brother Cameahwait the previous year. Clark and his men recovered the canoes and headed down down the Beaverhead, some in the canoes and some on horseback. They reached the Three Forks of the Missouri on July 13.

EXPLORING THE YELLOWSTONE RIVER

There Clark's party split. Sergeant Ordway and nine men in canoes headed back down the Missouri to the Great Falls to join up with the Lewis-led party. Clark and 12 others, including Charbonneau, Sacagawea, and little Pomp, set out on horseback to the Yellowstone. "The Indian woman . . . has been of great service to me as a pilot through this Country," Clark noted in his journal July 13, after Sacagawea helped guide Clark's group through a mountain pass (present-day Bozeman Pass) that she recommended to them as the best route to the Yellowstone valley. On July 19 they made camp along the Yellowstone at a site on the northern bank, south of present-day Park City, Montana. Clark would call this "Canoe Camp," because he set the men to work over the next few days fashioning two new dugout canoes.

Before the end of the trip, every member of the expedition had a landmark named after him or her. Perhaps the most widely familiar namesake is that of Pomp, Sacagawea's son. Clark named the 200-foot sandstone "tower" after the expedition's smallest member. *(Bureau of Land Management)*

Although Clark and his men saw no one en route to the Yellowstone River, Indians evidently saw them and their herd of horses. Half the horses disappeared one night, likely having become the property of the Crow Indians, who were renowned as some of the most skillful horse thieves among the western tribes. Clark decided to send Sergeant Pryor and three men on an overland journey with the remainder of their horses to the Mandan village, but on the second night, all their horses were stolen, and they had to hike back to the river. On July 24 Clark and the remainder of the party sailed down the Yellowstone in the newly constructed dugout canoes, the two lashed together so that they were less likely to overturn in the fast-running water.

On the following day, July 25, Clark's party came to a "remarkable rock" located on the north side of the Yellowstone. It was a 200-foot-high sandstone formation, which Clark named "Pompy's Tower" after Sacagawea's infant son. ("Pompy's Tower," located east of present-day Billings, Montana, has over the years become known as "Pompey's Pillar.") Before they left, Clark carved the words "Wm. Clark July 25, 1806" on the side of the rock— the most striking physical evidence that

This photograph shows a carving made by William Clark of his signature on July 25, 1806, in the side of Pompey's Pillar (Pompy's Tower), named after Sacagawea's son. *(Bureau of Land Management)*

remains today of the passage of the Corps of Discovery.

Clark's party reached the junction of the Yellowstone and Missouri on August 3. They were supposed to wait there to meet up with Lewis's party coming down the Missouri. By the next day, however, the presence of "excessively troublesom" mosquitoes, combined with the absence of buffalo, convinced Clark he should move his camp farther east along the Missouri. He left a note for Lewis attached to a discarded elk antler. On August 8 Sergeant Pryor and the three men under his command reached the Yellowstone's mouth. After their horses had been stolen, they returned to the river and constructed boats of buffalo skins stretched over a wooden frame, known as bull boats, and set off to catch up with the rest of the expedition. They saw Clark's note and continued on down the Missouri until they rejoined his party.

LEWIS'S ENCOUNTER WITH THE BLACKFEET

Back at Great Falls, Lewis divided his party. He left Sergeant Gass and five men there to wait for Sergeant Ordway and his detachment of nine men, who were coming downriver from Three Forks. The men at Great Falls would portage the expedition's supplies (including the precious journals) around the falls to the lower portage camp, where they would recover and put in order the white pirogue for the return trip to St. Louis.

On July 16, Lewis, George Drouillard, and Joseph and Reubin Field headed off on horseback along the northern edge of the Missouri, to intersect the Marias and then follow its course northward. Lewis knew this was a risky venture. They had already lost most of their horses to unknown Indians. The region around the Marias River, Lewis knew, was

home to the Blackfeet, the Indians who regularly raided and bullied the Shoshone and Nez Perce tribes. Thanks to their lucrative fur trade with the British in Canada, the Blackfeet were well armed by Prairie Indian standards. The Blackfeet were unlikely to look kindly on the coming of traders from the United States who might supply their enemies with a similar arsenal.

Keeping a sharp lookout for the Blackfeet, Lewis and his party arrived at the Marias on the evening of July 18. They headed upriver, and on July 21 came to a fork in the river. They chose to follow the more northerly fork, Cut Bank Creek. But it was not northerly enough: The river was bending westward. Arriving at "a clump of large cottonwood trees" on July 22, Lewis halted his party; from there, at a distance of about 10 miles, they could see that the river rose into the mountains, northeast of present-day Browning, Montana. They camped there that night at what Lewis named Camp Disappointment; he now had to admit to himself that the headwaters of the Marias "will not be as far north as I wished and expected."

Lewis and his men would have done well to head back to the Missouri as soon as they had seen that the Marias River was not the hoped-for highway to the Saskatchewan region. But Lewis had his men wait at Camp Disappointment for several days, hoping for the break in cloud cover that would allow him to take the accurate reading of the sky that would allow him to fix the location's longitude and latitude. On July 25, having come across signs of a recently abandoned Indian encampment, Lewis wrote in his journal "[W]e consider ourselves extreemly fortunate in not having met with these people." But their luck was about to take a turn for the worse.

The following day, July 26, Lewis and his men were finally heading back to the Missouri when they encountered "a very unpleasant sight": eight Blackfeet caring for a herd of about 30 horses. Lewis "resolved to make the best of our situation and to approach them in a friendly manner." He had his men approach the Indians on horseback, flying the American flag. The Indians were young men, some of them just teenagers, and they seemed as uncertain about the encounter as Lewis and his men were feeling. Reverting to the role of diplomat, Lewis handed out a handkerchief, a flag, and a medal to three of the young men he decided were "chiefs." Though outnumbered eight to four, Lewis decided his party "could mannage that number should they attempt any hostile measures." Using sign language to communicate, Lewis invited the Blackfeet to camp with them by the side of the nearby Two Medicine River, the southern fork of the Marias.

Once settled in camp, Lewis explained how he had traveled all the way "to the great waters where the sun sets." Along the way, he "had seen a great many nations, all of whom I had invited to come and trade with me on the rivers on this side of the mountain . . ." This was probably the worst thing Lewis could have chosen to say, since it let the Blackfeet know that their days of lording it over poorly armed enemies were about to come to an end, if these white strangers had their way. But for the moment all was peaceful. They smoked a pipe together, and Lewis invited them to accompany him down to the Missouri for a council. He stayed awake until all the Indians appeared to be asleep, and then he instructed Reubin Field to act as sentry and awaken him immediately if there were any sign of treachery or trouble from the Blackfeet.

Trouble came at first light the next day. Joseph Field had replaced his brother as sentry. Probably feeling drowsy, he got careless and laid his rifle down on the ground. One of the Indians, waiting for that kind of opportunity, jumped up and seized both Joseph and Reubin Field's rifles and ran off. Joseph woke up his brother and the two set out after him in hot pursuit. Reubin, who had picked up his knife, stabbed the thief to death.

Meanwhile, Lewis and Drouillard woke up in the commotion and found their own rifles being stolen by other Blackfeet. Drouillard wrestled his gun back from the Indian who had taken it. Lewis drew his pistol on the man who had his rifle, who threw it on the ground when Lewis shouted to him to drop it. Lewis told his men not to harm the Indian; one death was enough. But then other Blackfeet tried to drive off the whites' horses. Lewis and his men took off after them. Lewis pursued two of the Blackfeet until one of them stopped and hid behind some rocks. The other turned, musket in his hand, and apparently ready to shoot. Lewis got off the first shot, inflicting a mortal wound on the Indian who fell to the ground. But before he died, he propped himself up on one elbow and got off a return shot from his weapon at Lewis, who "felt the wind of his bullet very distinctly." The other Indian, armed with a bow and arrow, was still hidden in the rocks. Unable to reload his weapon because he had left powder and shot behind, Lewis made a quick return to camp.

Two of the Indians were now dead or dying, but the other six were still capable of fighting—or, worse, finding other Blackfeet to join them to seek revenge, not only on Lewis and his small band, but also the larger group that was heading down the Missouri. Lewis, Drouillard, and the Field brothers hurriedly gathered up what could be useful, including the flag Lewis had earlier given the Blackfeet. They burned the Indians' shields and weapons. Lewis left the peace medal he had earlier given the Blackfeet hung around the neck of one of the dead men, "that they might

Alert and on horseback with rifle in hand, the Blackfoot in this painting by Karl Bodmer (*A Blackfoot on Horseback, with Rifle*, 1833) shows that they would be a formidable adversary in battle. *(National Archives [NWDNS-111-SC-92842])*

be informed who we were," not quite the use for which the medals had been intended.

They mounted their horses and galloped off across the plains, covering nearly 100 miles before stopping at 2:00 A.M. on July 28 for a short rest. Lewis had not entirely forgotten the larger purpose of the expedition, even during these desperate hours. Pausing for a moment in midflight, Lewis had dismounted and picked a sample of the white-margined spurge, *Euphorbia marginata*—a species pre-

viously unknown to science. At first light Lewis and his men were back in the saddle, reaching the Missouri at midafternoon, where they had the "unspeakable satisfaction" of seeing 14 well-armed men of the Corps of Discovery heading down the river in the white pirogue and five canoes, with two others following on horseback. They abandoned their horses and continued on down the river together. They came first to the mouth of the Marias, where they dug up the cache of supplies they had left there. They had hoped to refloat the red pirogue, which they had left there the previous summer, but it turned out to be too badly rotted to be of any use. The white pirogue was now the last remnant of the fleet that began the Corps of Discovery's journey up the Missouri.

BACK ON THE MISSOURI

On August 7 Lewis and his men arrived at the confluence of the Missouri and the Yellowstone, but to their disappointment discovered that Clark was not there to meet them as planned. They found Clark's note, or at least part of it, still attached to the elk antler. They kept going, eager to reunite the expedition. But before they could do so, Lewis had another brush with death. On August 11 Lewis and Cruzatte were off hunting when Lewis's one-eyed companion mistook him for an elk and shot him in the buttocks. The wound was painful but not fatal. Lewis would travel most of the rest of the way down the Missouri lying on his stomach while his buttocks healed.

Mountain Men and the Fur Trade

Manuel Lisa was one of the St. Louis merchants who did business with Meriwether Lewis in the winter of 1803–04, and when the Corps of Discovery returned with stories of the wonders they had seen along the upper Missouri and the Yellowstone, he acted quickly. In 1807 he assembled an army of trappers, including several recruits from the Lewis and Clark expedition, and led them to the mouth of the Bighorn River in Montana. There they built a fortified fur trading establishment called Fort Raymond and started harvesting beaver furs. William Clark and the Chouteau brothers were investors in Lisa's profitable Missouri Fur Company.

Meanwhile New York merchant John Jacob Astor sponsored an expedition across the continent to the Columbia River in 1811, establishing Fort Astoria near its mouth on the Pacific. He organized a succession of profitable fur companies over the next decade and a half, building a trading empire that stretched from the Plains to the Rockies to China, where American furs found eager buyers. Astor became the nation's wealthiest businessman, thanks to the western beaver.

By the 1820s the western fur trappers were becoming popular heroes known as mountain men. Many of them, like John Colter, Jedediah Smith, and James Bridger passed into legend. While pursuing new trapping grounds, they came upon the geysers and hot springs of the Yellowstone region and the Great Salt Lake, and they developed the overland routes that tens of thousands of American setttlers would eventually follow to Oregon and California.

The triumph of the mountain men and the merchants who employed them came at a price. By the mid-1840s the western beaver population had been devastated by overharvesting, and the fur trade went into rapid decline.

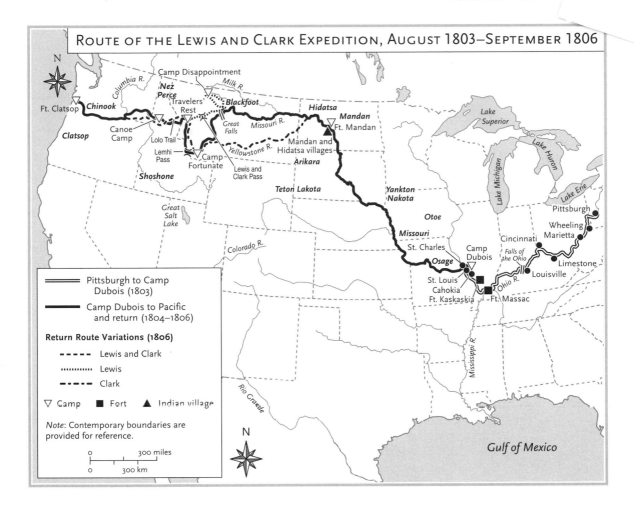

ROUTE OF THE LEWIS AND CLARK EXPEDITION, AUGUST 1803–SEPTEMBER 1806

The next day they met up with two white men, the first whites not in their party that they had seen since departing the Mandan village in April 1805. Joseph Dickson and Forest Hancock from Illinois had headed up the Missouri in August 1804 and spent two years hunting, trapping, and trading with the Indians. Dickson and Hancock told Lewis that they had met Clark the previous day, who was camped just a little farther downriver. Later that day, August 12, Lewis and his party caught up with Clark's group on the Missouri at a spot known as "Reunion Point," six miles

south of present-day Sanish, North Dakota. The Corps of Discovery, after many misadventures, was united and on its way home.

On August 14 they reached the Mandan villages. There they said good-bye, not just to the Mandan, but to Charbonneau, Sacagawea, and Pomp as well. Clark paid Charbonneau some $500 for his services. In his own mind, Clark may have thought the money should have gone to someone else in Charbonneau's family. A few days later he wrote a letter to Charbonneau, declaring, "Your woman who accompanied you that long dangerous and fatigueing rout to the Pacific Ocian and back diserved a greater reward for her attention and services on that rout than we had in our power to give her."

Dickson and Hancock, the two Americans that Lewis and Clark had encountered a week earlier on the Missouri, joined them at the Mandan villages. They asked John Colter to come with them on a fur trapping trip up the Yellowstone River, and the captains gave their permission for Colter to depart. Though it left four of its members behind on August 17 when it proceeded on down the Missouri, the Corps of Discovery had some additional companions for the rest of the trip. The Mandan

chief Sheheke and his family came with them to travel to Washington to meet the new Great White Father, accompanied by René Jessaume and his family.

As they continued down the river, they saw more familiar faces, welcoming the chance to renew their acquaintance with the Arikara and the Yankton Nakota, but angrily shouting at Black Buffalo and some of his Teton Lakota warriors when they saw them on the riverbank at the end of August. On September 4 they interrupted their trip to pay their respects to Sergeant Floyd where they had left him buried on a hillside overlooking the Missouri. The familiar sights of the lower Missouri

Given Up for Lost? ⟡

The last time anyone in the United States had heard from the Corps of Discovery was when they sent the keelboat down the Missouri from Fort Mandan in April 1805. Lewis had planned to send some of his men back later in 1805 with a further report on their progress along the upper Missouri but changed his mind. As months passed in summer and fall 1805 with no word from Lewis and Clark, rumors spread in the United States that the Corps of Discovery had all been killed or captured by hostile Indians or by Spanish authorities. In December 1805 Jefferson's friend Dr. Benjamin Smith Barton wrote to express his concern: "We are made uneasy here by a report, that Capt. Lewis and his party have been cut off. I hope this is not true."

So when the Corps of Discovery began to encounter other whites along the Missouri in September 12, they found themselves greeted as if they had returned from the dead. That day they met Robert McClellan, a former army scout who was now trading furs on the Missouri. McClellan was coming upriver in a keelboat with Pierre Dorion and Joseph Gravelines, both of whom Lewis and Clark had met on the river in 1804 and employed as interpreters. Clark noted in his journal that McClellan had been asked by American officials to "make every enquirey [inquiry] after Capt. Lewis my self and the party . . ." Sergeant Ordway reported in his journal that McClellan told them "that the people in general in the united States were concerned about us, as they had heard that we were all killed. Then again, they heard that the Spanyards had us in the mines . . ." Despite these fears, President Jefferson never gave up hope of Lewis and Clark's eventual return.

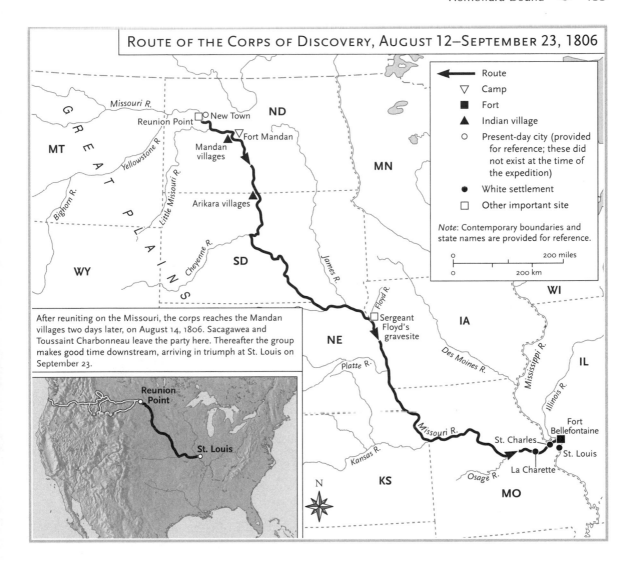

ROUTE OF THE CORPS OF DISCOVERY, AUGUST 12–SEPTEMBER 23, 1806

Legend:
- ← Route
- ▽ Camp
- ■ Fort
- ▲ Indian village
- ○ Present-day city (provided for reference; these did not exist at the time of the expedition)
- ● White settlement
- □ Other important site

Note: Contemporary boundaries and state names are provided for reference.

200 miles / 200 km

After reuniting on the Missouri, the corps reaches the Mandan villages two days later, on August 14, 1806. Sacagawea and Toussaint Charbonneau leave the party here. Thereafter the group makes good time downstream, arriving in triumph at St. Louis on September 23.

passed by rapidly, as they made progress up to 50 miles a day, better than three times their average mileage heading up the river in 1804. And, unlike their earlier trip, they now found the Missouri crowded with other travelers; before they reached the river's mouth they would encounter nearly 150 traders and trappers heading up the river. The Missouri was becoming a great highway into the Louisiana Territory, just as Jefferson had foreseen. They

picked up news from the travelers, and they also happily replenished their stock of flour, sugar, whiskey, and tobacco. And Lewis's wound was healing well; by September 9 Clark reported him all but fully recovered.

On September 20 they saw some cows on the shoreline, "a joyfull Sight to the party . . ." Clark noted, since it meant they had reached the edge of white settlement. In the late afternoon on September 21, they arrived in St.

Charles, where they were cheered, fed, and sheltered by the inhabitants who had seen them off in May 1804. On September 22 they traveled on to the newly established Fort Bellefontaine, the first U.S. Army post (apart from their own temporary forts) located west of the Mississippi. Their brother officers received them with full military honors, including a salute fired from the fort's guns.

The great moment of triumph came the next day, September 23: They proceeded on down the Missouri to its very end, made a quick visit to their old camp across the Mississippi, and then sailed back across the river to St. Louis. The city's inhabitants turned out on the shore and gave the Corps of Discovery three cheers as they came into view. The men clambered out of the white pirogue and the

canoes and carried their supplies to a storehouse. According to Sergeant Ordway, writing his last journal entry that day, the men "rejoiced" to find themselves safe and well at the end of the expedition, and with one common thought in mind: "[W]e entend to return to our native homes to See our parents once more as we have been So long from them."

It had been two years, four months, and 10 days since the Corps of Discovery set off in search of the Northwest Passage, a round-trip journey of roughly 8,000 miles. Lewis wrote to President Jefferson on September 23: "It is with pleasure that I anounce to you the safe arrival of myself and party at 12 Oclk.today.... In obedience to your orders we have penitrated the Continent of North America to the Pacific Ocean...."

Epilogue
Putting Their Names
on the Map

 Lewis and Clark and the men of the Corps of Discovery returned in triumph from their trip across North America, but it cannot be said that they all lived happily ever after—certainly not Lewis. At first, both captains enjoyed their newfound celebrity and its rewards. There were public celebrations, balls, and tributes in their honor, praise for them in the newspapers, important men who wanted to shake their hands, and significant financial rewards. By special appropriation, Congress voted to offer Lewis $3,600 in back pay, which was a sizable sum of money in those days, plus 1,600 acres of western land, which could be redeemed for an additional $3,200. Jefferson appointed Lewis governor of the Upper Louisiana Territory, which brought not only a steady salary but the opportunity to get in on the ground floor as an investor in the lucrative fur-trading enterprises that would soon exploit his discoveries in the Far West. Lewis also expected to profit from the sales of his account of the expedition, as soon as he

got around to rewriting the journals into a book. Clark reaped similar financial rewards, as well as an appointment as superintendent for Indian affairs for the Louisiana Territory, and as brigadier general of militia for the territory. In spring 1807, it seemed that both men, still in their 30s and in excellent health, enjoyed the prospect of long, honorable, and prosperous lives and careers stretching before them.

A LONG AND HONORABLE CAREER

For William Clark, that is the pretty much the way things turned out. His life remained closely bound to the territory he had explored. In 1813 he became the first governor of the Missouri Territory. He remained an honored figure both in Missouri and throughout the United States, and he even enjoyed international celebrity. Foreign dignitaries such as the Marquis de Lafayette came to visit him in St. Louis. Clark's private life proved as

155

This monument marks the grave of William Clark in St. Louis's Bellefontaine Cemetery, where he was buried after his long and successful post-expedition career. *(Library of Congress, Prints and Photographs Division [HABS, MO, 96-SALU, 84B-3])*

much a success as his public career. In 1808 he married Julia Hancock, the young woman also known as Judith for whom he named Judith's River in Montana. It was a happy marriage, and they had five children. In addition, Clark and his wife adopted Sacagawea's son Jean Baptiste—"Pomp"—and raised him as their own. They later assumed guardianship of another child born to Sacagawea and Charbonneau, daughter Lizette, as well as a boy, Toussaint, born to Charbonneau and his other Shoshone wife. Clark lived in St. Louis to the end of his days in 1838. He died in the home of his eldest son, Meriwether Lewis Clark, and was buried in St. Louis's Bellefontaine Cemetery. The monument above his grave bears the inscription "His life is written in the History of His Country."

A LIFE CUT SHORT

For Meriwether Lewis, things did not work out as happily. He proved an inept and unpopular governor of the Upper Louisiana Territory. He was unlucky in both love and business, beset by debt, and proved incapable of writing the account of the Corps of Discovery's expedition that he hoped would secure his fame and fortune. Out of despair, he started drinking heavily again. En route to Washington in fall 1811, he was overcome by depression. On the night of October 11, 1809, Lewis took his own life while staying at an inn in the little community of Grinder's Stand, Tennessee (southwest of Nashville). William Clark and Thomas Jefferson were grief-stricken to learn of Lewis's fate, but neither were surprised. "I fear O! I fear the weight of his mind has overcome him," Clark wrote on hearing the sad news. Lewis was buried near the inn where he had taken his life. The papers he carried with him en route to Washington, including the original field journals and maps of the Lewis and Clark expedition, were returned intact to Clark.

Painted shortly after the Corps of Discovery's return, this portrait of Lewis in an ermine coat and holding a gun depicts a self-confident, triumphant explorer, giving no hint of the desperation that would soon lead him to take his own life.
(Collection of The New-York Historical Society)

THE MANY PATHS OF THE CORPS OF DISCOVERY

The lives of other members of the Corps of Discovery were equally varied in their outcomes. Sergeant Patrick Gass would outlive Lewis, Clark, and everyone else on the expedition. A soldier in the War of 1812, he married at age 60, fathered six children, and lived on to 1870, when he died near to his 99th year. Several expedition members came to violent ends. George Drouillard and John Potts were both killed by Lewis's old foes, the Blackfeet, when they ventured back to Montana on fur-trapping expeditions, employed by Manuel Lisa's Missouri Fur Company. John Colter almost shared their fate. He was captured by the Blackfeet in the same incident in which Potts was killed, but the Indians decided to give him a sporting chance before killing him. They took all his clothes and let him run for his life. Incredibly, his feet torn and bloody, he managed to outrun his pursuers. It took him seven days of running to reach the safety of Manuel Lisa's fort on the Bighorn River, about 200 miles from his starting point. He died a peaceful death in Missouri in 1813. George Shannon was another expedition member who had a close encounter with death, shot in the leg in a hostile encounter with the Arikara Indians in 1807 while on a military mission up the Missouri. Though he lost the leg to amputation, he survived to become a lawyer and lived on to 1836.

The fate of other members of the expedition remains less certain. Some historical accounts report that York was given his freedom by a grateful William Clark for serving in the Corps of Discovery. But other accounts, and Clark's own letters, cast doubt on that particular happy ending. In one letter that Clark wrote to a brother in 1809, he complained about York's insolence and men-

Found in a Montana county named after Lewis and Clark, Helena National Forest (shown here) is a place where visitors can fish in the Blackfoot and Missouri Rivers and hike along the Continental Divide National Scenic Trail like Lewis and Clark did over a century ago. *(Library of Congress, Prints and Photographs Division [LC-USF34-065037-D])*

tioned casually that Clark "gave him a Severe trouncing the other Day and he has much mended."

As for Sacagawea, undoubtedly the most famous member of the Lewis and Clark expedition after the captains themselves, there are widely varying accounts of her later life. Some believe that she moved back to the Rockies and lived to old age, dying in 1884. The more likely account suggests that she died in December 1812 at Fort Manuel, a fur-trading post on the upper Missouri, shortly after bearing her second child. Her death was reported to Clark by an American fur trader, who called her "the best woman in the Fort."

The members of the Corps of Discovery died one by one, but their names lived on. Every single member of the expedition who traveled from Fort Mandan to the Pacific and back—including York ("York's Dry Fork"), Sacagawea ("Bird Woman's River"), and her infant son ("Pompy's Tower") had his or her name given to a river, an island, a bluff, or some other geographical feature the explorers encountered along the way. And in the two centuries that followed, people kept naming things after the explorers, as suggested by the names of the twin cities that lie near the confluence of the Clearwater and Snake Rivers, Lewiston, Idaho, and Clarkston, Washington. Sacagawea may have more places named for her than either captain, though with many variations in spelling: There is a Sacajawea State Park in Washington, a Lake Sakakawea in North Dakota, and a Sacagawea Spring in Montana. Larry McMurtry commented in a collection of essays on western history published in 2001 and entitled *Sacagawea's Nickname,* "[T]here are probably at least one hundred motels up and down the Missouri River named for Sacagawea . . ."

THE WEST SINCE LEWIS AND CLARK'S DAY

Much has changed in the landscape since Lewis and Clark's day, as those Sacagawea motels would suggest. There are interstate highways where once there were only dusty or muddy tracks on the land. The rivers have changed too. As Lewis's biographer Stephen Ambrose has written, "Today, Lewis and Clark would hardly recognize much of the Missouri River. The river is 127 miles shorter, one-third as wide, and far deeper and faster." The Missouri has been transformed for much of its length by dams, levees, and reservoirs. The Great Falls of the Missouri is no longer very great, as it is mostly covered by waters backed up from the Ryan dam. Many of Lewis and Clark's campsites in eastern Montana now lie beneath the waters of the Fort Peck Reservoir; the site of Camp Fortunate now lies under the waters of the Clark Canyon Reservoir. There are also four dams along the stretch of the Columbia River explored by Lewis and Clark (and even more farther upstream), and they have tamed and drowned Celilo Falls, and the Short and Long Narrows, as well as severely curtailing the salmon run on the river.

And yet there still are many places where visitors can see much the same view today as the one that greeted Lewis and Clark and the Corps of Discovery between 1804 and 1806, including the view westward from Lemhi Pass, or southward from Ecola State Park on Tillamook Head on the Oregon coast, or pretty much anywhere along the Upper Missouri, stretching 149 miles eastward from Fort Benton and designated as a National Wild and Scenic River.

The names of the Lewis and Clark expedition live on, as do at least some of the scenes of visionary enchantment they were privi-

leged to see. And so do their words. Lewis never produced his promised account of the expedition, and his failure to do so is a literary tragedy, because he proved himself in the journals a masterly writer. Clark found another writer to take on the task after Lewis's death, Nicholas Biddle of Philadelphia, who later went on to a distinguished career as a banker. Biddle's account, based on the journals, came out in 1814 as *The History of the Expedition under the Commands of Captains Lewis and Clark*. The journals themselves,

contained in 18 red leatherbound notebooks, were deposited in the archives of the American Philosophical Society in Philadelphia, where their existence was largely forgotten. Fortunately they survived nearly a century of neglect, and in 1904, on the expedition's centennial, a complete edition of the original journals was published, edited by Reuben Gold Thwaites of the Wisconsin State Historical Society. In the years that followed, other documents from the expedition turned up at irregular intervals. Sergeant Ordway's journal was not found until 1916; some of Clark's field notes turned up only in 1953. The latest edition of the expedition journals, including the writings of the enlisted men as well as the captains, was edited by Gary Moulton in a 13-volume edition that concluded publication in 1999.

THE PATH TO THE SEA

Their names survive, their words survive, and so do their contributions in exploration and

This photograph is a view of Tillamook Head as seen from Seaside, Oregon—the town that marks the end of the trail for the Corps of Discovery. *(National Archives [NWDNS-79-OC-2])*

This sign, one of many along the route, marks the area where the expedition reached the end of its westward trail, in Seaside, Oregon. *(Library of Congress, Prints and Photographs Division [LC-USF34-070422-D])*

discovery. Lewis and Clark did not find the Northwest Passage. They accomplished something greater. At a dinner in Lewis's honor held in Washington, D.C., in January 1807, the poet Joel Barlow read a poem he had written for the occasion. Barlow hailed the guest of honor as a "young hero" who taught the nation "his path to the sea." Americans would have found that "path to the sea" in time, even without a Lewis and Clark expedition. In fact, they would soon find shorter and better routes to the Pacific than the tortuous path that Lewis and Clark wound up following. What made Lewis and Clark true pathfinders was the impact they had on the American imagination. The journey of the Corps of Discovery established the destiny of the United States as a continental power, stretching from sea to sea. The *West,* that place existing largely as a blank spot on the map prior to 1804, became in the nation's imagination the *American West* after 1806. People could go there and come back. It had been done. It could be done again.

GLOSSARY

arid Dry, with little moisture.

bilious A medical condition thought to do with a malfunction of the liver, or the production of excess bile; a term also associated in the early 19th century with malaria.

botany The branch of biology that deals with plant life.

cache A hiding place in the ground for provisions.

cartography The design and production of maps.

chronometer An especially accurate timekeeper used to determine longitude.

climate Weather conditions of a region.

colic A pain in the stomach or bowels.

commerce Trade, business, the interchange of goods.

confluence A flowing together of two or more streams or rivers.

continental divide High ground dividing river systems that flow into different oceans.

corps An organized military body.

council A group of people assembled for consultation or deliberation.

court-martial A court that determines the fate of members of the military accused of violations of military law.

dialect A branch of a common language.

diplomacy The conduct of negotiations and other relations between separate states or nations.

dram A small drink of liquor.

dysentery An infectious stomach illness.

empire A collection of nations or peoples ruled by a single powerful central government.

epidemic A condition in which a single disease spreads rapidly among a large number of people.

espontoon (spontoon) An 18th-century infantry officer's weapon; a spear-headed brace that could be used to steady a rifle for more accurate firing. Lewis and Clark used theirs as a walking stick, rifle rest, and weapon.

estuary The part of the mouth of a river emptying into the ocean in which the river's flow is affected by the ocean's tides.

ethnography The scientific description and study of various human cultures and races.

headwaters The origin of a stream or river.

interpreter Someone appointed to translate what is said from one language into another.

keelboat A shallow freight boat used for river travel.

latitude The angular distance north or south from the equator of a point on the Earth's surface, measured on the meridian of the point.

longitude   The angular distance east or west on the Earth's surface, determined by the angle contained between the meridian of a particular place and the prime meridian in Greenwich, England.

meridian   A great circle of the Earth passing through the poles and any given point on the Earth's surface.

missionary   A person sent to spread his or her religious faith to nonbelievers, often in another country.

musket   A smooth-bored, muzzle-loaded firearm; the standard infantry weapon of the 18th and early 19th century.

naturalist   Someone engaged in the study of natural history, such as zoology and botany.

navigation   The art or science of directing the course of a ship.

paleontology   The study of forms of life existing in former geological periods, as represented by fossil remains.

pirogue   A small wooden watercraft. *Pirogue* is a French word that in the Canadian fur trade was used to describe a large dugout canoe. Lewis and Clark's "pirogues," however, seem to have been more on the order of a large, open lifeboat, flat-bottomed, with plank sides, and carrying a mast.

plantation   A farm or estate devoted to growing the kind of staple crops, such as cotton, rice, or tobacco, usually associated with warm climates.

portage   The act of carrying boats or goods from one navigable body of water to another, or the place where such things can be carried.

sovereignty   The supreme and independent authority of government to which others are subordinate.

tributary   A stream contributing its flow to a larger stream or body of water.

watershed   A high point of land dividing two river drainage areas.

zoology   The branch of the biological sciences that concerns the study of animals.

FURTHER INFORMATION

NONFICTION

Allen, John Logan. *Passage Through the Garden: Lewis and Clark and the Image of the American Northwest.* Urbana: University of Illinois Press, 1975.

——, ed. *North American Exploration.* 3 vols. Lincoln: University of Nebraska Press, 1997.

Ambrose, Stephen E. *Undaunted Courage: Meriwether Lewis, Thomas Jefferson, and the Opening of the American West.* New York: Simon and Schuster, 1996.

Appleman, Roy E. *Lewis and Clark: Historic Places Associated with Their Transcontinental Exploration (1804–1806).* Washington, D.C.: Government Printing Office, 1975.

Bakeless, John. *Lewis & Clark: Partners in Discovery.* New York: William Morrow & Company, 1947.

Betts, Robert B. *In Search of York: The Slave Who Went to the Pacific with Lewis and Clark.* Boulder: Colorado Associated University Press, 1985.

Biddle, Nicholas, ed. *History of the Expedition Under the Command of Captains Lewis and Clark, to the Sources of the Missouri, thence Across the Rocky Mountains and down the River Columbia to the Pacific Ocean. Performed During the Years 1804–5–6.* Philadelphia: Government of the United States, 1814.

Botkin, Daniel B. *Our Natural History: The Lessons of Lewis and Clark.* New York: G.P. Putnam's Sons, 1995.

Burroughs, Raymond Darwin. *The Natural History of the Lewis and Clark Expedition.* East Lansing: Michigan State University Press, 1961.

Brodie, Fawn M. *Thomas Jefferson: An Intimate History.* New York: W. W. Norton, 1974.

Calloway, Colin G. *One Vast Winter Count: The Native American West Before Lewis and Clark.* Lincoln: University of Nebraska Press, 2003.

Chuinard, Eldon G. *Only One Man Died: The Medical Aspects of the Lewis and Clark Expedition.* Glendale, Calif.: A.H. Clark Co., 1979. Reprint, Fairfield, Wash.: Ye Galleon Press, 1997.

Clark, Ella E., and Margot Edmonds. *Sacagawea of the Lewis and Clark Expedition.* Berkeley: University of California Press, 1979.

Crackel, Theodore J. *Mr. Jefferson's Army: Political and Social Reform in the Military Establishment, 1801–1809.* New York: New York University Press, 1987.

Criswell, Elijah. *Lewis and Clark: Linguistic Pioneers.* Columbia: University of Missouri Press, 1940.

Cutright, Paul Russell. *Lewis & Clark, Pioneering Naturalists.* Urbana: University of Illinois Press, 1969.

Coues, Elliot, ed. *History of the Expedition Under the Command of Lewis and Clark.* 4 vols. New York: Francis P. Harper, 1893.

DeVoto, Bernard. *The Course of Empire.* Boston: Houghton Mifflin, 1952.

DeVoto, Bernard, ed. *The Journals of Lewis and Clark.* Boston: Houghton Mifflin, 1953.

Dillon, Richard. *Meriwether Lewis.* New York: Coward-McCann, 1965.

Dramer, Kim. *The Shoshone.* Philadelphia: Chelsea House Publishers, 1996.

Duncan, Dayton. *Out West: A Journey Through Lewis and Clark's America.* 2nd ed. Lincoln: University of Nebraska Press, 2000.

Duncan, Dayton, and Ken Burns. *Lewis & Clark: An Illustrated History.* New York: Alfred A. Knopf, 1997.

Fanselow, Julie. *Traveling the Lewis and Clark Trail.* 2nd ed. Helena, Mont.: Falcon Press, 2000.

Fisher, Vardis. *Suicide or Murder? The Strange Death of Governor Meriwether Lewis.* Chicago: Swallow Press, 1962.

Furtwangler, Albert. *Acts of Discovery: Visions of America in the Lewis and Clark Journals.* Urbana: University of Illinois Press, 1993.

Gass, Patrick. *A Journal of the Voyages and Travels of a Corps of Discovery Under the Command of Capt. Lewis and Capt. Clark.* Minneapolis, Minn.: Ross and Haines, 1958.

Goetzmann, William H. *Exploration and Empire: The Explorer and the Scientist in the Winning of the American West.* New York: Random House, 1966.

Hawke, David Freeman. *Those Tremendous Mountains: The Story of the Lewis and Clark Expedition.* New York: W. W. Norton, 1980.

Hebard, Grace Raymond. *Sacajawea: A Guide and Interpreter of the Lewis and Clark Expedition.* Glendale, Calif.: A.H. Clark Co., 1957.

Howard, Harold P. *Sacajawea.* Norman: University of Oklahoma Press, 1971.

Jackson, Donald. *Among the Sleeping Giants: Occasional Pieces on Lewis and Clark.* Urbana: University of Illinois Press, 1987.

———. *Thomas Jefferson and the Stony Mountains: Exploring the West from Monticello.* Urbana: University of Illinois Press, 1981.

Jackson, Donald, ed. *Letters of the Lewis and Clark Expedition with Related Documents, 1783–1854.* 2 vols. Urbana: University of Illinois Press, 1978.

Josephy, Alvin M., Jr. *The Nez Perce Indians and the Opening of the Northwest.* New Haven, Conn.: Yale University Press, 1965.

Kessler, Donna J. *The Making of Sacagawea: A Euro-American Legend.* Tuscaloosa: University of Alabama Press, 1996.

Kroll, Steven. *Lewis and Clark: Explorers of the American West.* New York: Holiday House, 1994.

Lavender, David. *The Way to the Western Sea: Lewis and Clark Across the Continent.* New York: Harper and Row, 1988.

Long, Benjamin. *Backtracking: By Foot, Canoe and Subaru Along the Lewis and Clark Trail.* Seattle: Sasquatch Books, 2000.

Luebke, Federick C., et al., eds. *Mapping the North American Plains: Essays in the History of Cartography.* Norman: University of Oklahoma Press, 1987.

Madsen, Brigham. *The Lemhi: Sacajawea's People.* Caldwell, Idaho: Caxton Printers, 1979.

Malone, Dumas. *Jefferson the President, First Term, 1801–1805.* Vol. IV of *Jefferson and His Time.* Boston: Little, Brown, 1970.

McCracken, Harold. *George Catlin and the Old Frontier.* New York: Dial Press, 1959.

McMurtry, Larry. *Sacagawea's Nickname: Essays on the American West.* New York: New York Review Books, 2001.

Moulton, Gary E, ed. *The Journals of the Lewis and Clark Expedition.* 13 vols. Lincoln: University of Nebraska Press, 1983–1999.

———. *The Lewis and Clark Journals: An American Epic of Discovery.* Lincoln: University of Nebraska Press, 2003.

Murphy, Dan. *Lewis and Clark: Voyage of Discovery.* Las Vegas, Nev.: KC Publications, 1977.

Oglesby, Richard. *Manuel Lisa and the Opening of the Missouri Fur Trade.* Norman: University of Oklahoma Press, 1963.

Osgood, Ernest S., ed. *The Field Notes of Capt. William Clark, 1803–1805.* New Haven, Conn.: Yale University Press, 1964.

Peebles, John J. *Lewis and Clark in Idaho.* Boise: Idaho Historical Society, 1966.

Reid, Russell. *Sakakawea: The Bird Woman*. Bismarck: State Historical Society of North Dakota, 1986.

Ronda, James P. *Jefferson's West: A Journey with Lewis and Clark*. Monticello, Va.: Thomas Jefferson Foundation, 2000.

———. *Lewis & Clark Among the Indians*. Lincoln: University of Nebraska Press, 1984.

———. *Voyages of Discovery: Essays on the Lewis and Clark Expedition*. Helena: Montana Historical Society Press, 1998.

Ruby, Robert H., and Brown, John A. *The Chinook Indians: Traders of the Lower Columbia River*. Norman: University of Oklahoma Press, 1976.

Salisbury, Albert, and Jane Salisbury. *Two Captains West*. Seattle, Wash.: Superior Publishing Company, 1950.

Schmidt, Thomas. *National Geographic's Guide to the Lewis & Clark Trail*. Washington, D.C.: National Geographic Society, 2000.

Schwantee, Carlos, ed. *Encounters with a Distant Land: Exploration and the Great Northwest*. Moscow: University of Idaho Press, 1994.

Skelton, William B. *An American Profession of Arms: The Army Officer Corps, 1784–1861*. Lawrence: University Press of Kansas, 1992.

Snyder, Gerald S. *In the Footsteps of Lewis and Clark*. Washington, D.C.: National Geographic Society, 1970.

Steffen, Jerome O. *William Clark: Jeffersonian Man on the Frontier*. Norman: University of Oklahoma Press, 1977.

Thomas, Davis, and Karen Ronnefeldt, eds. *People of the First Man: The Paintings of Karl Bodmer*. New York: Dutton, 1976.

Thomas, George. *Lewis and Clark Trail: The Photo Journal*. Missoula, Mont.: Pictorial Histories Publishing Company, 2000.

Thwaites, Reuben Gold, ed. *Original Journals of the Lewis and Clark Expedition, 1804–1806*. 8 vols. New York: Dodd, Mead, 1904–1905.

Wilson, Charles Morrow. *Meriwether Lewis of Lewis and Clark*. New York: Thomas Y. Crowell Company, 1934.

Wilson, James. *The Earth Shall Weep: A History of Native America*. New York: Atlantic Monthly Press, 1999.

Woodger, Elin, and Brandon Toropor. *Encyclopedia of the Lewis and Clark Expedition*. New York: Facts On File, 2004.

FICTION

Glancy, Diane. *Stone Heart: A Novel of Sacajawea*. New York: Overlook Press, 2003.

Hall, Brian. *I Should Be Extremely Happy in Your Company: A Novel of Lewis and Clark*. New York: Viking Press, 2003.

Lasky, Kathryn. *The Journal of Augustus Pelletier: The Lewis and Clark Expedition, 1804 (My Name Is America)*. New York: Scholastic, 2000.

Myers, Laurie. *Lewis and Clark and Me: A Dog's Tale*. New York: Henry Holt and Co., 2002.

Thom, James Alexander. *Sign-Talker: The Adventure of George Drouillard on the Lewis and Clark Expedition*. New York: Ballantine Books, 2001.

Roop, Connie, and Peter Roop. *Girl of the Shining Mountains: Sacagawea's Story*. New York: Hyperion Press, 1999.

WEB SITES

Go West Across America with Lewis & Clark. Available on-line. URL: http//www.nationalgeographic.com/west. Downloaded on June 6, 2003.

Lewis and Clark Education Project. Available on-line. URL: http://yoda.cec.umt.edu/lewisclark. Downloaded on June 6, 2003.

Lewis and Clark National Historic Trail. Available on-line. URL: http://www.nps.gov/lecl. Downloaded on June 6, 2003.

Lewis and Clark Trail Heritage Foundation. Available on-line. URL: http://www.lewisandclark.org/index.htm. Downloaded on June 6, 2003.

Lewis and Clark on the Information Superhighway. Available on-line. URL: http://www.lcarchive.org/fulllist.html. Downloaded on June 6, 2003.

INDEX

Page numbers in *italics* indicate a photograph. Page numbers followed by *m* indicate maps. Page numbers followed by *g* indicate glossary entries. Page numbers in **boldface** indicate box features.